ENJOYING

A LIFETIME

IN YOUR OWN

HOME

A GUIDE TO AGING IN PLACE

PAULA FUOCO, RN, BSN

Enjoying a Lifetime in Your Own Home

Paula Fuoco, RN, BSN

Printed in the United States of America

ISBN: 9781075089398

*To my husband Ron
and my daughters Lisa and Allison.
Thank you for your encouragement.*

TABLE OF CONTENTS

INTRODUCTION

Paula Fuoco is an RN with a bachelor's degree in nursing who worked in the field for more than 30 years. During her time as a nurse, she discovered a need for alternatives for people who want to return to their homes after a hospital stay.

Throughout her years in nursing, she encountered thousands of patients in hospitals, homes and clinics in several areas of the country and has seen people in their most vulnerable states. Fuoco provided care to acutely hospitalized patients specializing in cardiology and interventional cardiology. She also delivered in-home care including dialysis, IV infusion, wound care and education for self-care in the home. Her case management responsibilities included several specialties: orthopedics; ear, eye, nose and throat; neurology; nephrology; and oncology. All these specialties revealed similar results. Patients often ended up in a nursing home without having expected it and their lives were turned upside down.

Developing repeated contact with patients with severe chronic conditions, she saw panic and disbelief when their health conditions quickly became "acute on chronic." She watched as patients advanced such chronic conditions including cardiac disease, stroke, diabetes, cancer, and kidney and liver failure that led them to enter a nursing home unexpectedly. People who were expecting a simple procedure ended up in "skilled nursing facilities" instead of going home.

Fuoco saw most people accepted the need for lifestyle changes due to their chronic conditions and made the required incremental adjustments in their daily lives. But, when complicated by something as simple as a fall, situations became dire and often people didn't realize it was going to lead them away from their home. It is warranted to say that many people reject facing these situations. Moved by the huge gap in their accepted wisdom, Fuoco found many patients were left to think about aging somewhere other than in their own home. Subsequently, most patients simply failed to see the giant leap which placed them into an institution.

Many people that Fuoco has spoken with have given this issue little thought. It appears, when they feel when the time is right, they can make that decision. However, most circumstances do not lend themselves to forethought. The usual situation is one of being thrust into a forced decision in which one is not prepared. Very rarely has she seen someone waking up at home and deciding it was time to go to a nursing home.

After years of bedside nursing, when her career evolved into case management, developing feasible discharge plans and future management for these patients became her focus. This is when Fuoco saw the aftermath of the hospital recovery.

The choices are often slim: long-term acute care; acute inpatient rehabilitation; skilled nursing facility (nursing home); versus skilled visiting nurses and/or physical therapy (home care); or self-care at home if the situation was deemed safe.

From her experience in home care, Fuoco could predict, with solid evidence, who would thrive and who would fall into institutional care at some point. Hospitals, in general, refused to accept liability for what they considered "unsafe discharges." She found one common denominator in phrases that inspired this book.

"I never thought I would live to this age."

"How did I get here? And, what do I do now?"

"I just want to go home."

"I don't want to go to a nursing home."

With witnessing the experiences of others desperate to stay in their own home, Fuoco desired to tell people how they could avoid being unwillingly displaced. This book is full of individual stories, methods for staying in your own home for as long as possible, and ways to proactively plan as you age.

May you be able to live your life to the fullest exactly how and where you want.

1

A TYPICAL HOSPITAL EXPERIENCE

"During the summer we lived in our home in Michigan, but during the winter we spend a few months in Arizona."

~ Marie- a typical patient~

Angelo and his wife Marie were in their late 70's and retired. They looked forward to their annual trips to Arizona. It was a good way to enjoy great weather year-round and avoid the hard Michigan winters. They had purchased a home there years ago when the prices were favorable.

"The journey has become a regular part of our life and we looked forward to it every year," said Angelo.

Every day was like being on vacation for Angelo and Marie. They leisurely began their days with a homemade breakfast and a cup of coffee. Then they walked laps around the neighborhood for their morning exercise with their dogs. They talked for long hours about life and their future together. Family was the center of their universe. Since their primary residence was in Michigan, they called home at least three times a week, typically later in the day. Angelo and Marie had two grown children. Both children had full-time jobs and families of their own.

Angelo and Marie had visited Arizona many times before. Even though they walked their dogs every day they never really made contact with the neighbors. The houses were distant from each other. They had each other and they made Arizona their private oasis. Besides, they had a very rich entourage of family and friends in Michigan. Winter was a time for them to be together without the distraction of social responsibilities.

On one very typical day, Marie did not get up at the usual time. The dogs were anxiously waiting for their morning walk. Angelo had already woken up and thought he would let Marie sleep a little longer since they stayed up late to watch a movie the night before. But before long, the dogs did not want to wait. They were clamoring to go out.

So, Angelo went to check on Marie to see if she had gotten up yet. He was shocked to find her on the floor in the bathroom. She seemed to be trying to talk to him but couldn't quite get the words out. He knew something was seriously wrong. As he tried to lift her, he realized that he did not have the strength. Her body was limp. She desperately tried to tell him what happened, but her speech was garbled, and she was confused.

Angelo decided to call for the emergency medical services and dialed 911. As he was waiting for the rescue, it seemed like time had slowed down to a crawl. Angelo was concerned that he and Marie lived remotely enough that the emergency services may have had a difficult time accessing their property. But they had gotten there quicker than Angelo had realized because they knew the area and had gone to homes there frequently. The shock of finding Marie on the floor had panicked him so much that time seemed to stand still.

Also, getting to the hospital seemed like slow-motion. He joined Marie in the ambulance and watched her get increasingly disabled in her speech and orientation. Never imagining that this could happen on their vacation, Angelo felt helpless and in disbelief.

After arriving at the hospital, time sped up into a whirlwind. The doctors and the nurses swiftly moved Marie through the assessment and evaluation of her condition. Her CT scan revealed that she had a left-sided stroke. The clotbusting drugs were able to be given because, luckily, the treatment time window for tissue plasminogen activator (TPA) had not passed.

Ordinarily, these drugs should be given within a three-hour window of the start of stroke symptoms. This usually means the patient is found within a short period of time following the onset of initial symptoms and a quick trip to the hospital is required to receive the treatment in a timely fashion. If administered quickly, the medication can prevent or even reverse the effects of a stroke.

Angelo was overcome by panic and a wave of incredulous thoughts.

"I never expected this to happen," said Angelo. "How could she go from being so healthy to having a terrible stroke so quickly? She is very healthy, she exercises, and she eats well. I don't think she has high blood pressure and I haven't seen any recent signs of problems. This can't possibly be happening."

Within seconds, Angelo saw his beloved wife and partner slipping away. Marie still could not speak, and her body had no strength. Angelo knew that life for them had changed in this instant and he was in shock.

"What am I going to do? I don't know anyone here in Arizona," thought Angelo. "I don't have help. I hope she's going to be okay. I'm so glad I was there, and we got to the hospital on time. What do I do now? I don't want to leave her. I need to call someone for help?"

Angelo immediately called their children. Receiving a call from their father so early in the day was a shock for them. Both of their children were working at the time. One of their adult children wanted to rush to Arizona to help. The other adult child could not leave at that time because she had recently started a new job.

Their oldest son, Jack, was trying to arrange a flight to Arizona. He already knew this scenario from a previous fall his mother-in-law had taken. His experience with the repercussions of a stroke worried him. He knew that his mother-in-law had never fully recovered. With this in mind, Jack tried to book a flight to Arizona as quickly and as reasonably priced as possible. Without at least two weeks' notice, it would cost him a substantial amount of money to make the trip.

Thoughts flooded into Angelo's mind so fast. Within a few hours their whole lives had changed. Even though they were in their late 70s, they were always very healthy, and a stroke did not seem like a possibility at all.

"I felt so alone and there was nothing I could do to help her," said Angelo. "I sat by her bedside as the clot-busting medication was infusing and kept staring at her waiting for something to happen. She seemed very sedated. I know she was given medication to keep her calm, but she looked like a different person. I wanted to stay there and never leave."

Unfortunately, Angelo needed to continuously run back and forth to the house to care for the dogs.

"I wish I knew someone closer to help like a neighbor or friend," said Angelo. "But I had to call my son and make him book a flight to Arizona. I called Jack because I knew he would come. However, the last thing any parent wants is to be a burden on their children. When I saw her lying there and unable to speak, I feared things would never be the same and I would need help."

Within just a few short days, Marie started to look a little better.

Her speech was improving but she still looked differently to Angelo. She said a few words but sometimes they didn't make sense. He was very excited when she recognized him and was able to say his name. Her right side was extremely weak, and her mouth was drooping. She wasn't taking in much food or drink. These changes left Angelo feeling a sadness that he had never known before.

In those few days in the hospital, she had been seen by several doctors and nurses as well as a specialist. She was also seen by a variety of therapists including a physical therapist, an occupational therapist, and a speech therapist, all of which had evaluated her. She had also endured a slew of tests.

"I was barely able to pay much attention to everyone and their role," said Angelo. "All I saw was our lives unraveling. The reality of the future at home was daunting. An RN case manager came to our bedside as well."

The RN case manager offered the discharge plan that was recommended by the therapists and the specialists based on the results of Marie's evaluation. Within five minutes, the RN case manager had asked some basic questions and handed Angelo a list of facilities. It turned out that Marie would need much therapy and the lists revealed names of skilled nursing facilities.

The RN case manager stated that the therapists determined Marie was not strong enough to do the three hours of therapy required at an inpatient rehab. She would need a less intense program of a skilled nursing facility or "SNF" (often called sniff by those in the medical profession) for short. Skilled nursing facility was the contemporary euphemism for "*nursing home.*"

"I was dumbfounded," said Angelo. "I never expected to hear those words, 'nursing home.' We had been both healthy and vital. This can't be happening. I can't believe that they would try to send her to a *nursing home*. We can do better than this. *I want to take her home.*"

At that moment, Angelo knew that their lives had changed forever. He rejected choosing a skilled nursing facility, a nursing home, or any institution. The case manager handed him a list of facilities but, he did not know where they were or what they provided. She explained that this facility would likely be a short-term detour towards home.

Angelo was not so sure, considering her present debility. He wrestled with the potential outcome of entering a nursing home.

He definitely knew that this was not their plan.

"I requested another assessment by the physical therapist," Angelo said. "I watched as the therapist transferred her to a chair with a gait belt (a belt that is put around a patient to help lift them up)."

The verdict was the same. Marie's right side was far weaker than her left. Her speech, her swallowing, and her memory were also an issue.

"Where had my wife gone?" wondered Angelo. "I was faced with choosing a nursing home for my wife and I didn't have much time. The discharge papers arrived that day."

Angelo wanted to stall this process. He knew Marie did not want to go to nursing home, but he also knew that signing out against medical advice would be an *insurance nightmare*. Angelo and Marie's son had also arrived, and Angelo called him to quickly set up some help at home. Angelo then frantically asked the therapists if homecare was an option and they gave him the basic information he needed.

"The RN case manager came back to see us, and I explained that I would like to care for Marie at home," said Angelo. "We had a long discussion about the risks and benefits of taking Marie home. Convincing the case manager that I was prepared to care for her safely at home was my primary goal. I assured her that I could be there for her safety all day. Much of the equipment that we needed would be purchased despite the cost."

Angelo's sales pitch was successful. The plan was to discharge Marie to home with nursing, speech, and physical and occupational therapies. He was fortunate to have the resources to obtain what was needed to safely take Marie home. The RN case manager was satisfied that Marie would have a safe discharge and was willing to set up home care for her as a result. She informed Angelo that getting all the services he would need for Marie would be a challenge due to their remote location and their insurance had limitations regarding home health. Angelo forged ahead despite this news; however, his work was just beginning.

Upon discharge, Angelo found he was barely able to transfer Marie into the car. Marie was heavy and unable to completely assist with her movement. She helped with all her strength because they were in agreement to get home. The trip was difficult. When they got home, they needed a wheelchair to get her into the house.

The steep slope of the driveway was never so intimidating. Since their son was there, it made a big difference in helping Marie successfully transition home. They needed to hastily buy some equipment: a wheelchair, a walker, and a raised toilet seat with handrails. Angelo then had to remove all the barriers to prevent falls. They rented a hospital bed. The costs were adding up. It was apparent their lives would never be the same. Angelo just maintained hope to take one step at a time, literally.

"Even with the two of us there, it was exhausting," Angelo said. "I wanted my wife back and I wanted my life back. I would do whatever I could to get her there."

The therapists came two to three times a week for one hour and the nurse came once a week. As they struggled through the days, Marie needed much more than Angelo could have imagined. He chased her intense, aching pains with positioning and medication. Anything he could do to make her comfortable was on the table.

Once the pain was manageable, things improved. The transferring to and from the bed to the bathroom became easier as Marie gained strength. Angelo was still very concerned, however, that taking Marie home may not have been the best choice.

"Marie wanted to be home and I wanted her to be home," said Angelo.

Angelo could provide Marie with consistent therapeutic exercises. He had been told the risks of going to a skilled nursing facility/nursing home were high. A nursing facility would only provide one hour of therapy a day and the risk of severe infection and complications were high.

Besides, Angelo estimated, the comfort of one's own home could not be matched. Their independence as a couple continued as they set their own schedules for eating, sleeping, and enjoying leisure time together. They invited visitors during their preferred time. He wanted Marie to know that they would always stay in their home no matter what. Angelo knew these were her wishes also.

Coordinating visits from different therapies and nursing became Angelo's new job. Twenty-four hours a day, Marie would need him. Their son, Jack, was very helpful during his visit. Arrangements were made by him for equipment and readying of the house. Jack knew that he had other responsibilities at home in Michigan and would not be able to stay for very long. What should have been a marathon of preparation had become a sprint of panic.

"I was feeling a little guilty burdening him with these responsibilities," said Angelo, "but I knew he was as devoted as I was to help his mom."

Activities of everyday living required Angelo's energy and exertion to the point of exhaustion. He knew Marie needed him and he was determined he would continue to care for her. But he found himself wishing he had made plans before this happened. Even though they were in their late 70s, they had never really thought about altering their home or needing a caregiver.

"We always wanted to enjoy every day together in our own home," said Angelo. The thought of going to a nursing home was devastating and it came without warning.

"I was very fortunate that we had some help and available resources to bring her home," said Angelo. "And I know once you go to the hospital, you lose a lot of control of your future. *The hospital is very resistant to discharging anyone unsafely.* So, luckily my sales pitch was convincing though I knew we were not ready."

Angelo realized this *was* going to be a 24-hour workday. He had to quickly hire help throughout the night. His days were spent practicing therapy with Marie. Angelo learned to cook. He learned body mechanics for transferring and how to use a walker. He learned how to put on her makeup and fix her hair.

"I wished I had some medical knowledge because I struggled to replicate the discharge teachings," said Angelo in hindsight. "I saw Marie smiling as she progressed, and she was able to converse with me better."

With the diligence of the therapists and Angelo's constant attention, Marie was able to recover at home.

"In my opinion, she made approximately an 80 to 90 percent recovery," Angelo said. "Being unprepared made the experience extremely stressful, both emotionally and physically. Our lives had changed dramatically. When the bills came, I became an expert on health insurance. Tests, doctor's visits, and medication have become part of our new reality. What is co-insurance? What constitutes a deductible? What am I getting for my monthly premium? I learned a new vocabulary including terms such as DME (durable medical equipment) and I knew where to find it."

Despite his ability to learn quickly and care for Marie, this was not the way Angelo had expected their lives to be.

"In my secret thoughts, I always pictured Marie as *my* caregiver," Angelo said. "And I found, through support groups which I now attend, that this was common among husbands. I have a new sense of preparedness and appreciation. I am grateful to have my wife back."

Angelo said he wished that he and Marie had known about these common realities as they aged. He wished they had been more realistic about their future.

"When I looked back on this experience, there were so many factors that could have made this an easier adjustment," he said. "I underestimated the gravity of this possibility in our lives. Luckily, we had our son to lean on. But the social aspects of our lives in Arizona, I had overlooked. We had such a full life in Michigan with family, many friends, and neighbors. Here, when we needed support, we had no one locally that we knew well enough to ask for help. I wish that we had built more substantial relationships in Arizona. I believe we failed to do this because we considered ourselves to be 'snowbirds' as our 'real' home was in Michigan."

The costs were great with both the social isolation and financial stress. Marie had always taken care of their finances. Angelo found he was at a loss in the ability to access money which he needed for this emergency. He drained much of their checking account when he could've been using their health savings account (HSA). The HSA they had was specifically set up for such medical costs, but he didn't know. Angelo had also spent money on things that would have been paid for by their insurance.

"Marie and I have discussed our finances in the past," said Angelo. "Though, I relied on her entirely too much in this area and I was disorganized, especially with the details."

While Angelo and his son were busy with Marie's physical recovery, their spare moments were spent sifting through an organized, yet somewhat chaotic list of computer passwords and important documents.

"I had logged onto many of our shared accounts previously, but I never practiced navigating the sites. Many hours of aggravation and emotion could have been erased for me if Marie and I had truly shared this responsibility," said Angelo. "Looking back, there are many things I could have done differently. We were fortunate to have made it through this experience. I guess this is just another part of lifelong learning that we needed to maintain our planned independence."

A Note from the Author

"A Typical Hospital Experience" shows us the commonalities of stressors created during thousands of scenarios I have seen. Unexpected medical and life events have thrown families into chaos and started a chain reaction which set them on a course towards acceptance.

According to the book *On Death and Dying: What the Dying Have to Teach Doctors, Nurses, Clergy, and Their Own Families* by Elisabeth Kubler-Ross (1969), she famously delineates the five "stages" of loss and grieving as: denial and isolation, anger, bargaining, depression, and acceptance. In the book, she also meticulously describes the emotional states seriously ill people commonly experience and the adaptive mechanisms. As you read this account, you saw Angelo and Marie address similar phases in this life-changing experience as they headed towards the acceptance phase.

Lifelong learning and experiences do not end at retirement.

Maintaining your independence requires many things. In hindsight, Angelo and Marie realized that they were unprepared for this life-changing journey. In the rest of this book, you will find all the needed elements to *"Enjoy a Lifetime in Your Own Home."*

2

PEOPLE FIRST & RENEWING

RELATIONSHIPS

The desire to age in place comes with the great assumption that life will go on uneventfully. After all, our homes are our sanctuaries and there seems no reason that we should ever have to leave them. As an RN who has seen patients in every setting, I have heard people say, "Under no circumstance would I leave my home "or "You would have to drag me out."

Beginning with suppositions that we will remain in our homes forever can conclude with the exact opposite results. Oftentimes, the decision to leave our home may be beyond our control without proper planning. This chapter and the following chapters offer realistic preparations to conquer these assumptions and overcome possible challenges.

According to *Aging in Place: A State Survey of Livability Policies and Practices*, a 2011 study by the American Association of Retired Persons (AARP), "Nearly 90 percent of people over age 65 want to stay in their home for as long as possible, and 80 percent believe their current residence is where they will always live. However, for older adults to age in place, their physical and service environment must be accommodating (2011)."

We each choose our homes for good reason. When we decide to select a home, it's because there is something special about it. It is your welcoming, comfortable, place to settle into at the end of the day. Home is the base that grounds you to a foundation of familiarity with friends and neighbors. Whenever you work or travel, the urge to return home eventually falls upon you. Especially in times of crises, home provides stability.

Relationships are an imperative part of maintaining your independence as you age. Social isolation can lead to depression, especially in times of stress. It is not good for your mental or physical health and can contribute to many health issues that take you out of your home.

"Being alone most of the time is associated with increased weight, poorer diet, decreased exercise, alcohol abuse, greater risk of sickness, and even a shorter life span. Cognitive functions decline, possibly as a result of few verbal interactions," according to an article in *Psychology Today* (Wurtman, 2017).

As a case manager, I knew that a patient who lived alone signaled a major red flag. They had a much greater chance of needing extra care, possibly in an institution. Many times, there was a frantic search for someone to help them with the responsibilities they left at home so abruptly. They may have pets to look after. They may have some things to set up in their house for their return home. Since such a crisis had taken place in their life, maybe they just need someone to talk to for advice. Family is usually the first choice.

"It is Possible"

Below, you will find personal stories of those who cherish their homes and independence. The goal of reading their narratives is to better understand the circumstances that landed them where they ended up and offer you guidance in your own age planning.

Sophie and Helen

A noisy city in a neighborhood of multilevel row homes and busy streets awaited me, their visiting nurse. I drove up to a free space and parked myself there for most of the day. Walking past trash cans set on uneven surfaces, I thought this place was least likely to house an older person thriving alone.

Yet there she was, waiting at the bottom of her stoop, outside in the cold. Sophie, 72, pale and thin, invited me into her second story duplex. On the way up the stairs, she carefully climbed between the bags on both sides and maneuvered like a pro. Sophie was blind.

"My father left us this house," she said. "It will always be our home." Sophie spoke often about her sister, Helen, who lived downstairs. Neither had ever married so they occupied this house, each staking out a floor for themselves.

My goal this day was diabetic teaching. Sophie's blood sugars were frequently out of control as she was a brittle diabetic. Her vision was severely impaired by the diabetic rampage on her body. Sophie's goal, however, was to prove to me her happiness and joy in her abilities despite her disabilities.

She managed her home in a steady chaos, created to suit her blindness. She cooked with the bare necessities in an established kitchen design. By living in a city, she accessed public transportation. Visiting nurses, like me, were available to her for medical maintenance. I provided all her equipment and teaching to keep her on track. Her greatest asset was her determination to remain home, in the city where she felt connectedness and security from an early age.

Despite their rivalries, Sophie melded relations with Helen, who lived downstairs, so she had support in overcoming the barriers which she faced with the help of her sister. Regardless of my presence, arguments ensued between them daily. Helen was an alcoholic and sat for most of her days. She lifted herself from depression and addiction by caring for her sister. An unlikely pair, their relationship sustained them. It broke the self-centered trap and isolation of addiction for Helen who supplied groceries and clothing for Sophie. Helen also aided in the financial management of their inheritance from their father. She became functional enough to keep an orderly household.

Sophie and Helens' symbiotic success story was born of necessity despite their vast differences. It was not the best of relationships, but it worked for them both.

The Grandmother

In one instance I was involved with as the case manager in the hospital, I remember family members fighting amongst each other to take "Grandma" home with them. Grandma had such great relationships with all her family members, children and grandchildren, she could not decide. Her two daughters each had a different plan for her to come to their homes. As a case manager, they each presented to me a plan to better manage Grandma at home. There was such a strong family bond, and everyone loved Grandma so much that there was dispute over this.

Ultimately, Grandma had to make the final decision. It was always the patient's choice that overruled everything. Her two daughters were trying to recruit her to come to each of their homes. One daughter was offering her own room and her own bathroom. The other daughter was offering the care from her grandchildren in addition to herself. As a case manager, I was thrilled to see such a loving family and I knew that this grandma was going to be fine with whichever choice she made.

There came a point when I needed to ask the daughters to leave the room so Grandma would feel free to make a choice. And once

Grandma made a choice to stay with one daughter, the other daughter immediately offered to come to her house and help. I could see the love in this family and the genuine compassion for Grandma. And I only wish that everyone had this great connection.

A Story of My Own

I recently made a trip back to visit my own family. Most of them live a very long distance away. The trip was significant because I was going to set up resources for my own parents. They were aging and my mother had been diagnosed with dementia. They needed assistance and as a nurse and her daughter, I was happy to help.

Unexpectedly, I found an enormous amount of family members whom I had not seen in years. It is strange that you can pick up a conversation where you left off years ago. Many of us were living parallel lives on different coasts. It did not take very long to revive the relationships we had. In addition, I met new family members with whom I could continue to bond as they grew. The trip was a success for reasons beyond which I had imagined. You'll hear more about my own story later in Chapter 7.

A Nurse's Perspective

As a nurse, I was always excited to see so many people in a room with a patient. When I entered a room and I could not find the patient because there were 12 people around the bed. When this was the case, I knew that this patient had a great chance of returning home.

Despite their circumstances I felt that at least one of those people in the room would be the primary caregiver. Sometimes there were so many people in a room visiting, I could not get to the patient. The love of some families was so strong that every cousin, grandchild, sister, brother, spouse, and ex-spouses would show up to support the hospitalized patient.

This was expected in certain cultures, but many times in our transient society, it was also a result of the other great support they had in their lives. Either way, it was exciting to see that so many people cared. As a result of touring the room for support people, I assessed the unspoken family dynamic. I could then receive answers to my assessment questions.

My typical questions as a case manager focused on getting the patient home. I asked several questions. Where do you live? Who do you live with? Are they helpful to you? Do you have any equipment at home? Do you use any outside services? Do you have any barriers to your care, physical or otherwise? Do you have transportation? What is your desired plan for discharge?

The strength of family connections was evident by the visitors. If they were able to answer questions quickly for the patient, I knew they were involved. I was especially surprised to see the benefits of pairing the young and the old. The knowledge and experience of an older person creates wisdom for the younger generation. Younger generations can learn responsibility in caring for their older relatives.

Family Bonds

When I brought up the topic of living a lifetime in your own home, I was overwhelmed with stories similar to those above. "My mother-in-law moved in with us last summer," "My father needed some help and we cared for him," "My grandmother was left in the big house when my grandfather passed away, so we moved in to help her." The stories go on and on in the same fashion.

In times of crisis, families jumped in to assist older generations.

These incidences led to great upheavals in family homes. But in most cases, a family's strong ties melded into a stronger multigenerational bond.

There are many ways that you can build a family support system and renew relationships. The most obvious way to build relationships and have a trusted person in your life is to rely on family. Parents or children can step in to help easily because they know your needs. Sisters and brothers close by also can be a great help because of their similar ages.

But this is often easier said than done. Relationships within families are sometimes strained. Family bonds and loyalties wax and wane. But, ultimately, most families pull together in times of crisis.

Living alone, especially without assistance, can lead to serious consequences including an increased chance of ending up in a skilled nursing facility. A study published in the *Journal of General Internal Medicine*, "Problems of Older Adults Living Alone After Hospitalization," concluded that "Patients who live alone and receive home nursing after hospitalization are less likely to improve in function and more likely to be admitted to a nursing home, compared with those who live with others. More intensive resources may be required to continue community living and maximize independence (Mahoney, Eisner, Havighurst, Gray, & Palta, 2000)."

The benefits of having a close family include familiarity, geographic proximity, and anticipation of the other's needs. In times of crisis or sickness, family members are usually the first people who will be present to help. Most families are quick to step up to responsibilities. They can care for dependents at home, physically and financially. Family members usually have a bond which supersedes any other support system.

In modern American society many people have become distant from their families. It may be a geographical separation. It may be an emotional distance due to miscommunication and resentments. But I have seen many family members drop everything and fly across the country to help their loved ones.

Many times, a family member may move in with someone to care for them. Ultimately, they may need to relocate and change their lives completely to focus on their family member. Family connections are strong. Family is always the first line of defense because of the unspoken love and obligation to care for each other.

Making Connections and Reconnecting

If you haven't already begun to do so, start connections with your family. It is important to nurture those relationships. Attend family functions such as weddings, birthdays, and perhaps a traditional weekly meal.

Nurturing relationships requires work and a give-and-take attitude. Even a relative whom you've had little contact with can be found through social media. Many applications and programs search ancestry. Search engines exist to look up names and addresses. I think you would be surprised that much of your family would be excited to reconnect with you.

We are very lucky to have social technology to keep ties with our family. For example, Facebook and Skype are available. Instagram and Snapchat make it easy, too. The lists for connections through social media are endless. Even if you lost ties with your family over long periods of time, relationships can be renewed without the awkwardness of a face-to-face meeting. Social media provides a more comfortable avenue to start, or restart, a conversation. There are resources available to help you learn to use these social networks. This is discussed in depth later in this chapter.

Prepare to devote time and energy in building trust in your family. Supporting family bonds strengthens the most significant people in your life. The first step is the hardest. Thriving rather than merely existing for a lifetime in your own home is a journey of exploration with no boundaries.

Friends Are the Family We Choose

The need for friendship in life cannot be underestimated. Friends frequently offer support which family members are unable to match. The reasoning behind this; you choose your friends based on compatibility. No specific rules apply. The bond between friends carries strength.

"A real friend is one who walks in when
the rest of the world walks out."
~Walter Winchell

The National Center for Biotechnology Information published a study by John T. Cacioppo and Stephanie Cacioppo in the U.S. National Library of Medicine National Institutes of Health titled "Social Relationships and Health: The Toxic Effects of Perceived Social Isolation" found loneliness to be associated with ill health to a greater degree than just social isolation. Stronger relationships were shown between loneliness and worse health in the study including cardiovascular disease, inflammation, and depression. Loneliness in older adults was shown to significantly increase risk of functional decline and death in a recent longitudinal cohort study of 1,604 people followed over six years (Cacioppo & Cacioppo, 2014).

Friends

No one can predict where their next friendship will develop. Support systems can emerge from other sources as well. I have had patients with very close friends and neighbors. These friends and neighbors likely had access to the patient's homes. They were familiar with the patient's habits and responsibilities.

Sarah

One patient I can remember had an extremely close friend. Sarah had an unexpected accident that that affected her vision. She needed multiple eye drops in both eyes every two hours. She was not able to see well enough to administer these herself. If it were not for her friend and neighbor, she would have likely not returned home.

It seemed like an insignificant problem to administer eye drops but the patient could not manage on her own, especially with around-the-clock scheduling needs. Her neighbor was willing to come to her house every two hours and administer these drops. As Sarah recovered, the frequency of the drops decreased. Within two weeks the drops were discontinued. Because of the diligence of her neighbor and their close relationship, Sarah left the hospital early. She comfortably maneuvered around her own home without the fear of the unfamiliar environment of the hospital.

Laura

Laura was probably the best prepared for her situation. Even though she lived alone, she anticipated that she would have needs in the future. She bought a townhome in a gated community which was set up for an over 55 crowd. Laura was an optimistic, forward-thinking woman.

Independence was always a goal for Laura. After her divorce, she was alone for many years. Her children lived out of state but, even at the age of 76, she was still driving a convertible Mustang and attending social gatherings all over town. Laura was very realistic about her needs as an independent woman.

The deep friendships that she nourished throughout her solo years gave her as much comfort as family. She also volunteered to help others and was always willing to jump in at a moment's notice. It seemed she was always on the phone with someone and her calendar was always full. Her living arrangements at home were also accommodating for friends to visit and socialize. Many of her friends were of similar age to her own.

Laura's townhome was on one level and it had a great-room with an open floorplan. Her bathrooms had level, walk-in showers and grab bars. Her doorways to the bathroom in the bedroom were wider than usual, about 36 inches. She also felt more secure in a gated community.

When Laura needed a hip replacement, she knew the course of her treatment in advance. Luckily, her hip arthritis was chronic, and she was able to plan her surgery. But, knowing her, I felt that she was so proactive in her own life, even an acute event would not have derailed her. Laura was just continuing with the happy, healthy life she had always had. Her attitude throughout her life was forward-thinking so any bumps in the road were flattened by her positivity.

I was always envious and somewhat baffled by her happy spirit.

Laura was very proactive in her life in all areas. Enjoying a lifetime in your own home should be a natural continuation of your present lifestyle and Laura made this look effortless.

Once she finished her surgery, she would need three hours of therapy a day. She was always very active, and her health was good enough for her to do this intense therapy. For two weeks she spent time in acute inpatient rehab. She had chosen this rehab beforehand and knew that it had a good reputation. Even though she spent some time rehabilitating as an inpatient, Laura knew that her home would be ready when she returned.

Her friends visited her often during her rehabilitation and her recovery at home was very successful. She needed only a cane and she was still able to drive. Her townhome set up made it a flawless transition for her to return home and her many friends helped her with everyday activities which would have been a challenge. Laura happily remains in her home still today.

Not every story flows as effortlessly as Laura's. As a visiting nurse I have seen hundreds of older people living in their forever homes comfortably. Despite their situation, a proactive approach and a good support system can make any situation doable. A little planning and a little forward thinking can make a life-changing event into a less stressful, natural part of life.

Making Friends

Now that many people live distantly from their families, friends are more important than ever. There are many avenues towards making friends. Start locally with neighborhood watch groups and homeowners' associations. If you really want to be involved with your neighbors, have a block party. Share food and exchange addresses and phone numbers.

Another good way to start the process of developing friendships is to walk your neighborhood. Say hello to your neighbors when you pass them. Use neighborhood chat rooms if you are not comfortable in person. Offer services and trade useful belongings which could be shared via neighborhood chat rooms. An abundance of applications exist to facilitate neighborhood connections. For example, *Nextdoor* is an app solely designed to connect you with *your* neighborhood. You have much in common with your neighbors and they can become trusted friends.

Expand your circle to enhance your hobbies, likes, and dislikes. Many local churches have *Bible* studies. They display bulletin boards for activities in your local area. Some churches even provide specific support groups. Many areas also have senior centers where people gather to play cards, take courses in computers and the arts, or even go on trips together.

To expand your relationships even further, support groups especially are a prime source of making deep-lasting connections. Most true friendships develop when people share experiences that no one else can understand. Somehow these experiences bond friends in a way that supersedes other relationships. Support groups exist for everything. Any specific issue will bring people together to support one another. There are support groups for divorce, debt, addiction, cancer survivors, veterans, grieving, transplant patients, and the list goes on. You can easily find support groups online.

For most extroverts, socialization comes naturally. However, introverted persons may need to make an extra effort. It may be easier for an introvert to simply volunteer. Volunteering for things that embellish your life will reciprocate in the future. You will be able to make fast friends without an uncomfortable effort. If socialization is uncomfortable for you, volunteering offers an easier way to make friends that share the same interests.

As an introverted person, I have expanded my social circle through hobbies and sports groups. You can find sports teams to join at your local gym. Likely, there are also sports and hobby groups available that are sponsored by your community. Local community colleges offer infinite possibilities as well. Whether you are a spectator, a fan, or an active participant, sports and hobby groups are everywhere.

Even if you are not involved with many social situations at this time, start now. There is always room for something new in your life. Brainstorm a quick list of at least 10 items for your" bucket list." What would you like to try? Here are some ideas to get you started:

- Biking
- Hiking
- Golf
- Cycling
- Volleyball
- Swimming
- Horseback Riding
- Team Sports
- Knitting
- Gardening
- Painting
- Sculpting

- Reading
- Walking/Hiking
- Fan Groups
- Pet and Animal Organizations
- Online Classes
- Online Dating
- Online Gaming
- Chat groups
- Exploring New Technology
- Traveling
- Writing a Book
- Block Parties
- Political Organizing
- Churches
- *Bible* Study
- Check Bulletin Boards in Your Local Area
- Meet Up Groups
- Volunteering
- Part-Time Work

This list should be enough to get you started in terms of thinking about building a network of friends. Social networks and trusted friendships can push through all the barriers of living a lifetime in your own home.

Assess your current situation. Is there someone you could call in an emergency? Conversely, are there people in your life for whom you would be available in a moment's notice? Reciprocity, common interests, and a willingness to both give and receive assistance can make friendships strong and long-lasting.

The process towards enjoying a lifetime in your own home is built on a foundation that parallels your life as it is now. The way you live and the friends you enjoy now should naturally flow into your future spent at home. This begs some questions. Are you willing to accept help from people? Are you willing to give help when someone is in need? If you have difficulty with relationships and friendships, now is the opportunity to change your interactions with the world. Close and trusted friends and family make the difference in how you will be loving life.

Another benefit of having a social circle is referrals. When you live in your own home there are many needs to address. Your friends, family, and neighbors can provide referrals for you for personal care, home renovation, and many other needs. Personally, I would trust the opinion of a friend or family member when hiring someone more than I would trust a stranger online writing a review. When people are coming into your home, you want to make sure they are safe and reliable. Become an active participant in your life and in that of others.

Village to Village Networks

Village to Village networks consist of groups of individuals with a common goal of assisting older Americans who wish to age in place. "Villages," as they are called, allow people to more easily stay in their home by focusing on the services they need to do so. According to the Village to Village Network website, the "Village Movement" began with the Beacon Hill Village in Boston more than 15 years ago. These villages are becoming more and more popular and are popping up throughout the United States with more than 200 Villages now in existence. In America alone, there are more than 150 that are in development today.

"In 2010, the Village to Village Network – a national organization that collaborates to maximize the growth, impact and sustainability of individual Villages and the Village Movement – was formed," according to the network website. "The Network provides expert guidance, resources and support to help communities establish and maintain their Villages. Village to Village Network and the Village Movement will not only impact

Villages and their members, but the lives of countless families, caregivers and members of the broader community they serve."

A large, compact city such as Boston was an unlikely setting for accommodating an aging population. However, these groups focus their services on older Americans with gaps to fill in their home care and they are wildly successful in doing so. Mimicking the assistance of a retirement community, the "villages" provide transportation, landscaping, yard work, bookkeeping and many other services.

According to a 2011 article by Martha Thomas on the AARP website, "Villages: Helping People Age in Place," members pay an annual fee with an average of about $600 for a variety of the aforementioned services. The piece points out that there are typically only one or two paid employees in a village that act as a liaison or concierge that direct members to volunteers for support such as younger neighbors, youth groups that conduct community service projects, or even other able-bodied village members. The concept of community is evident by combining the local skills of each generation.

"Villages also provide lists of approved home-maintenance contractors, many of whom offer discounts to members," according to Thomas's article. "By relying on this mix of paid and volunteer help, members hope to cobble together a menu of assistance similar to what they would receive at a retirement community, but without uprooting their household."

You can find "Villages" in your area by visiting the Village to Village Network online at vtvnetwork.org as well as additional resources.

Social Media

Regardless of your age or of your parent's age, you and/or your parents can learn to use the Internet and social media. Even if the Internet seems like a foreign language to you, you can learn to use it very easily. You can access an infinite amount of information on the Internet and getting involved with others online will increase your social network 100-fold. This is especially true if you are homebound. Social networking can take you into a new society of friends.

As with any other circle of friends, social media allows you to find others with common interests. Research topics that interest you and mimic your current social life online. All the social groups that are listed above can also be found online. There are groups for any topic that you can name. If you cannot find the topic that you are looking for, you can always start your own blog to draw in others that are like-minded and make new connections.

Joe, 72, a widower, whom I have known for a long time, was an avid bicyclist. He spent a great deal of time road cycling every week with his dedicated group of friends. Even though he has fun, close relationship with these friends, he found himself still lonely without his wife.

At 72 years old, Joe decided to try online dating. He was shocked to find many people his own age involved with online dating. Even though Joe was not socially isolated, it was difficult for him to find that special partner. He researched the online dating sites for a long time before he actually sent a message to anyone. This was a new experience for him, and he was reluctant to trust. He had heard all the rumors about online dating, and he knew it was not his usual mode of operation.

Nonetheless, he tried it. He met someone with whom he had a connection. Eva, 69, was also a widow and she lived about an hour away. After conversing for at least a month, they decided to meet at a bicycling event midway between their residences. Though Eva had a history of road cycling and was very interested in continuing the sport, she was not able to participate in the event, so she cheered for Joe from the sidelines. After the event, they were able to get to know each other in person and had long conversations.

What had started as an online conversation developed into a very happy relationship. My friend Joe, and his newfound friend Eva, were married within a year. Eva took up cycling on a three-wheeler and joined Joe's cycling club when she moved into his home. I don't think Joe or Eva ever expected that this relationship would have evolved online. The possibilities of relationships through social media truly exist and I have seen it firsthand.

In addition to building new relationships online, social media can also rekindle relationships. Facebook, Skype, Twitter, Instagram, Snapchat and other social media applications enable us to instantly follow the day-to-day happenings in the lives of all of our friends and family. I have personally reconnected with many old friends and family members online. I can update, at my fingertips, the daily events of my life to share with others as well. At any other time in history, we would not have been able to so easily find these past relationships.

If you or your parent are unfamiliar with the Internet, go to your children or your grandchildren. They are excellent resources that can fill you in on its use. Many local community colleges, municipalities, and senior centers also offer technology courses for a fee or for free so you can learn to use the internet and social media.

Staying current with technology allows you to stay current with your family and friends. The interfaces are becoming easier with each passing week and, as I will discuss in future chapters, navigating the Internet will become an invaluable tool to staying in your own home.

On this note, I would like to include that college-age students are an invaluable, untapped resource. Many universities require volunteer hours for credit and pairing the young and older generations is a win–win situation. Students obtain credit for classes while older generations can benefit from the socialization. Students can summarize technology quickly and can practice their study skills. Transferring their knowledge to older people teaches them to interact in real life.

It is never too late to start something new. Friends, family, neighbors, and support groups strengthen our happiness and allow for the exchange of ideas and growth. Other social interaction such as hobbies, athletic organizations, and church groups offer a chance to enrich your life. Social media has expanded our opportunities to grow in our relationships with others more than we have ever been able to in the past.

I encourage you to build relationships, nurture others in your life, and continue current connections. This chapter reflects on the continuation of your current social interactions. It also allows you to expand your social network to build loving relationships for a lifetime. Please reflect on the people in your life at this time and also consider new avenues to form connections. Social interaction and connections with other people are probably the most important part of your journey towards enjoying a lifetime in your own home.

After hearing these success stories, I noticed the commonalities which contribute to enjoying a lifetime in your own home. The most successful people who flourished at home for their lifetime *always* had a support system in place.

When I worked at the hospital as a case manager, I felt an immediate relief when someone told me that they had someone at home caring for them. This gave me the first insight towards a discharge plan. *Having a support system was invaluable.*

When a crisis happens, such as a hospitalization, your thoughts typically quickly change to deal with the immediate events. How did this happen? What should I do? What will happen to me? Who could I call to take care of my responsibilities at home? Sometimes you just feel lost.

The most successful people who enjoy a lifetime in their own home continue daily interactions with the people they love. This is the reason that a full life at home depends on others. It is not a change from your regular life, nor is it a situation where you should be isolated.

Whether or not you anticipate a hospitalization, successful recovery depends on a support system. The best support systems are comprised of people who naturally gravitate towards helping others as well as your willingness to accept help. Success in enjoying a lifetime in your own home is greatly increased with a willingness for give and take.

Most success stories have a back story. These back stories include a lifetime of relationships that did not rely solely on family or friends. People who are successful at home have typically maintained *a strong social support network* including continuous relationships which flourished. Maintaining relationships is sometimes difficult but is a very important factor in having a successful, full life at home. Relationships with family and friends require cultivation.

3

YOUR IDEAL HOME &
A TIME TO REDECORATE

While approaching the subject of aging in place, I was faced with some anxiety. This may have stemmed from some denial on my part. While denial is a factor for most people, it seemed odd to me that this should occur given that we lay groundwork for other periods of our lives.

Starting as early as grade school, we equip ourselves to perform our best. We progress into high school and beyond without giving much thought to our preparations along the way. The learning curve towards adulthood seems natural.

But, as adulthood marches on, less and less planning is focused on new stages of our journey. I'm sure some of this thinking is fueled by advertisers to perpetuate youth; however, this leads to a diminishing celebration of lifelong experiences. These experiences should empower us to value the need for preparation towards our goals and a seamless transition into our later years.

I began thinking of this transition as a positive opportunity to redecorate my home. By far this was the most exciting part of my journey toward enjoying a lifetime in my own home. Anticipating the chance to redecorate and remodel was the ideal way to create the perfect environment for ease of living. Simplicity and functionality were key in this area. Adding my sense of style and creativity was a bonus.

After an unanticipated trip to the hospital, the need for the process of adapting your home will be evident. Proving to the hospital case manager, therapists, and nurses that you will have a safe home environment is crucial. The choices for therapy could lead you to a nursing home, rehab facility, or long-term care. Hospitals are required to safely discharge patients according to the recommendations of therapists and physicians. The hospital, generally, does not want to take risks of unsafe discharges. Unsafe discharges jeopardize their insurance coverage, liability insurance, and good standing with regulatory agencies.

Mimicking your status when coming home from the hospital will be necessary to evaluating your home. Consider the trip home from the hospital. You will most likely be tired because you have been sleeping in a hospital bed. You may have equipment you need to take home with you as well. Even the transition from the hospital bed to the wheelchair and then to the car may be exhausting. Hopefully, you'll have someone to help you with this journey.

When you arrive home, everything will be different. The home that welcomed you after a vacation may not be so welcoming after a hospitalization. Some of the issues you may be dealing with are pain and weakness. You'll also need to consider the durable medical equipment such as wheelchairs, walkers, and canes that you may need when you arrive home. These issues, compounded by your past medical history (PMH), may add to your frustration. Many people go to the hospital due to an acute episode of a chronic illness so issues such as balance, stiffness, and weakness may also be multiplied.

Also keep in mind that the person bringing you home may not be a usual caregiver. Their stress level is probably elevated as well.

This is a new experience for them also so preparing your home will make the process a gentler and easier transition towards your recovery.

A Closer Look at *Your* Home

Assessment is always my first consideration as an RN in a hospital setting. In your home setting, you will also need to conduct an adaptability assessment. This will require multiple walk-throughs of your home. In order to diagnose your home environment, you will need some diagnostic tools.

Before you begin, I need to preface these walk-through activities by warning you to do this at your own risk. If you are unable to take this risk in any way, defer to a safer alternative. For example, AARP.org provides a free HomeFit Guide. It helps with the room by room assessment of your home (AARP, 2019). If you give this book as a gift, consider performing the assessment for the recipient.

For starters, recruit an agile victim, whether yourself or someone else, to suit up with some boots, slippers, or oversized shoes to mimic neuropathy and impaired balance. Balance problems or other injuries may impair ambulation. An alternative to these would be a wheelchair. Both options are advised due to the unpredictability of your future needs.

During a separate walk through, wear glasses (shaded or soaped) and gloves (preferably garden or winter type) to simulate visual impairment and incoordination. In yet another walk-through, gently place ear buds in your ears to mimic hearing impairment. Please ensure you have hands-on assistance during these walkthroughs for safety reasons.

Don these items separately to assess your home and begin at the front entrance, garage door, or both. Use all your senses to address immediate barriers there. At the entrance, consider your feelings. How difficult is opening the door handle and simply walking in? Are there steps leading up to your entryway? One of the first questions the case manager and/or discharge planner will ask you is, "Do you have stairs in your home?"

Now, slowly, consider the path of least resistance. Are there barriers? Is there clutter? Do you have uneven surfaces or tripping hazards? This is difficult to imagine preemptively, but it is a very effective success strategy for enjoying a lifetime in your own home. As you move through your home, it will be clear where your barriers lie.

Make your way to each room and assess which areas are most appealing, both functionally and aesthetically. For example, as I started the first walkthrough, I noticed the dim light and blandness of color. Suddenly, through my shadowy vision, I immediately decided that bright light and colorful aesthetics were more necessary to me than I had realized. Lighting was a huge safety factor.

As you conduct each of these walkthroughs, remember to use all your five senses to assess. We heavily rely on vision and hearing. Thus, sights of blurry pets at your feet and muffled sounds from unknown sources are scary. Lack of sensation in fingers and toes predicate injury. Odors can make you short of breath. Tastes of ill-prepared meals with incorrect ingredients are also examples of surprises you may encounter.

The Bathroom

Now, move on to activities of daily living or, in hospital terms, ADL's. The ADL's include hygiene, bathing or showering, and shampooing. Dressing can be added to the list as well as toileting. Practice and practice again. Repeat over several days to assess thoroughly.

In this area it may be necessary to remove some of your assessment garb. Please remember to focus on safety throughout this process. Most falls occur in the bathroom. Your private sanctuary will become very public if you fall.

The bathroom is a focal point of most ADL's. Were you able to enter the bathroom effortlessly? Were your ADL necessities within reach? Did you have to struggle to reach for every item? Could you see well enough to maneuver around unexpected items? Were you able to access your clothing and undergarments? Were you obstructed in any way to make an all-important quick trip to the toilet? Simply entering and maneuvering to the bathroom may be an issue when you first arrive home following a hospital stay.

Most adults use the bathroom at least five times a day. Practice your morning routine. Shaving, showering, and shampooing are challenging enough especially if you are not a morning person like me. Getting ready to start your day with ease initiates a successful, productive one.

Another thing to consider is whether you share bathroom space. Is everyone in your house mindful of the others' abilities? Share your experiences with your family following your walk through.

While wide doorways and shower bars are common in newer homes, it's not necessarily the case with older ones. If you have an older home, don't move walls or start demolition. There is often an easier way. The strength of an older home's character need not suffer for functionality.

Conducting this activity enabled me to see the true potential of my own home. Dressing in character made it real. Most of all, when I was finished, I got to redecorate with purpose. My designs would be a double investment in both my personal style and functionality as I age in place.

Besides overall general maneuvering, I was surprised by the effort of the little things. For example, I found my hands were fumbling to put on makeup with standard brushes and I could not see the results. My sink was too low for continually reaching down and washing my face, especially with a walker in my way. The shower handles were difficult to grasp. Even tearing off sheets of toilet paper was frustrating. I prefer to not even discuss the effort of getting up from a low toilet.

Immediately, I knew remodeling was inevitable for my bathroom (as I secretly hoped it would be). Yours may require less attention. The beauty of the assessment is finding the hidden strengths which your home already possesses. Keep in mind that the results of home remodeling/redecorating will provide true pleasure for a lifetime. Everything in life is fluid and the investments in your home now will also reap benefits for future generations.

The Bedroom

Most needs will be obvious, but one very important element for health and happiness is often overlooked. Sleep is so vital to recovery and stress relief after a hospital experience. Check your sleeping quarters for distraction, comfort, and safety.

Practice getting in and out of bed. Is it easy transferring from a wheelchair into your bed? Is your mattress firm and low enough so that you don't slide off? Are you able to see and feel items by your bed which you may need during the night? What about lighting? Was it at a safe level of brightness? Quality sleep is something to cherish while recuperating in your own home. No institution can provide the sweet restfulness of your own quiet bedroom.

The Kitchen

In addition to sleep, the common denominator to all survival and pleasure is food. Meal preparation is a secondary, yet important ADL. Cooking and food preparation for yourself and/or others encompasses many skills. These skills will be challenging for a recovering person.

Scan your kitchen. Are the foods accessible and identifiable? What about utensils and cookware? Are you able to reach all your essentials? Are they placed randomly or in a designated space? Are you able to open the doors to your cabinets? Are you able to access your appliances? Did you expend too much energy bending and lifting? Practice many methods of cooking and recipes you savor. Focus on the pleasure and ease of cooking in your kitchen.

Are your ADL's compromised?

Daily functioning with slippers, gloves, earmuffs or goggles is not as easy as your may imagine. After hospitalization, these activities replicate your potential challenges. If your home is set up safely, you can recover there safely and without risk of complications from an institutional environment. Keep in mind, hospitals are *required* to safely discharge patients according to recommendations of therapists and physicians.

Looking Ahead

Ashley, a registered and licensed Master's level occupational therapist, assists orthopedic and neurologically impaired patients in an acute care rehabilitation hospital in effort to prepare them to return home. While physical therapists deal with large motor skills and help patients get from one place to another, occupational therapists are more specialized.

The role of an occupational therapist is to deal with all the patients' needs when they get arrive back at home including their ADL's such as dressing, showering, and toileting. These are the most crucial activities to make patients successful at home.

"These things are often underrated," Ashley said of the importance of occupational therapy. "When you get home from the hospital, your first hurdle will be your activities of daily living."

When it comes to preparing your home as you age, Ashley said the best place to start is in the bathroom. She suggested grab bars and nonskid stickers as an easy fix. Ashley said that you should remove all the flooring items that may cause toe jams and tripping hazards. You can purchase easy-grab soap, shampoo bottles, brushes, and other utensils. She said other overlooked items that are helpful are nonskid, easy-on shoes and slippers.

Beyond small changes in the bathroom, Ashley said patients who are serious about staying in their own home need to research universal design.

"Universal design is a very hot, new trend which incorporates accessibility for all ages in a household," she said. "Many homebuilders are now considering this design in new home plans. They are taking into account the aging population and the need for multi-generational living."

Universal Design

Universal design focuses on more specific accommodations for private residences. It accounts for the needs of every family member from infants to the elderly. This is especially important in families where several generations live together and share space.

"Universal design is a framework for the design of living and working spaces and products benefiting the widest possible range of people in the widest range of situations without special or separate design" (Rossetti, 2006). There are seven principles of universal design that should be considered when designing a home that works for everyone and considers everything from appliances to furnishings for your home.

"Principle One: Equitable Use- The design is useful and marketable to people with diverse abilities" (Rossetti, 2006).

- "It provides the same means of use for all users: identical whenever possible; equivalent when not."
- "It avoids segregating or stigmatizing any users."
- "Provisions for privacy, security, and safety are equally available to all users."
- "The design is appealing to all users."

You may live alone or share your home with others. You need to consider your home as a whole functioning unit for people of all abilities as well as yourself. The principle of equitable use makes consideration for your recovery needs and the needs of others in your home. These designs consider various needs for every member of your family and a universally designed, equitable-use home should flow effortlessly for all who live there.

"Principle Two: Flexibility in Use- The design accommodates a wide range of individual preferences and abilities" (Rossetti,

2006).

- "It provides choice in methods of use."
- "It accommodates right or left-handed access and use."
- "It facilitates the user's accuracy and precision."
- "It provides adaptability to the user's pace."

When it's time to redecorate your home, you have a chance to show your individual style. You can incorporate ease and functionality within your home without eliminating your creative personality. Take advantage of the wide variety of your favorite things and incorporate them into your fluid and purposeful home design.

"Principle Three: Simple and Intuitive Use- Use of the design s easy to understand, regardless of the user's experience, knowledge, language skills, or current concentration level" (Rossetti, 2006).

- "It eliminates unnecessary complexity."
- "It is consistent with user expectations and intuition."
- "It accommodates a wide range of literacy and language skills."
- "It arranges information consistent with its importance."

- "It provides effective prompting and feedback during and after task completion."

One of the skills I learned when working with patients and their families is that we must teach to the lowest common denominator. This may sound trite, but this manner of teaching is all-inclusive and constantly encourages a person in the group who is more experienced to offer their skills to someone of less experience. This also holds true when it comes to universal design. Thus, the simplest and most intuitive design pleases everyone. The nature of the universal design is one that is effortlessness and safe for all members of the household despite their abilities.

"Principle Four: Perceptible Information- The design communicates necessary information effectively to the user, regardless of ambient conditions or the user's sensory abilities" (Rossetti, 2006).

- "It uses different modes (pictorial, verbal, tactile) for redundant presentation of essential information."
- "It provides adequate contract between essential information and its surroundings."
- "It maximizes 'legibility' of essential information."
- "It differentiates elements in ways that can be described

(i.e., make it easy to give instructions or directions)."

- "It provides compatibility with a variety of techniques or devices used by people with sensory limitations."

As you move through your home with your assessment garb. you will probably notice the severe impairment of your senses. This principle of universal design anticipates the needs of all levels of sensory perception. As we and other members are our family age, we need to be mindful that our senses may be diminished. Universal design takes into consideration the need to effortlessly move through our homes and function well. Our home will become an asset to our lives as we age in place.

"Principle Five: Tolerance for Error-The design minimizes hazards and the adverse consequences of accidental or unintended actions" (Rossetti, 2006).

- "It arranges elements to minimize hazards and errors: most used elements, most accessible; hazardous elements eliminated, isolated, or shielded."
- "It provides warnings of hazards and errors."
- "It provides fail-safe features."
- "It discourages unconscious action in tasks that require vigilance."

In "A Typical Hospital Experience" from chapter 1, we saw Angelo and Marie struggle after her stroke and subsequent fall. Falls at home are a prime cause for hospitalization in an aging population. Universal design principle number five is paramount to minimizing accidents, falls, and overall hospitalizations for this reason. As you assess your home, you can find and eliminate your own potential hazards. Welcoming safe places make your home a comfort to all generations.

"Principle Six: Low Physical Effort- The design can be used efficiently and comfortably and with a minimum of fatigue" (Rossetti, 2006).

- "It allows user to maintain a neutral body position."
- "It uses reasonable operating forces."
- "It minimizes repetitive actions."
- "It minimizes sustained physical effort."

Considering principle six, low physical effort, leads me to focus on the idea of recovery after hospitalization. If your goal is to return home, then you will need a balance of energy and restfulness. This is especially true during the stressful time of transition back into your home. Any design that reduces your physical effort will leave room for the regeneration of your body.

This may be a temporary or long-term need, but, nonetheless, it is important to enrich your life in your own home as you age.

"Principle Seven: Size and Space for Approach and Use-Appropriate size and space is provided for approach, reach, manipulation, and use regardless of user's body size, posture, mobility" (Rossetti, 2006).

- "It provides a clear line of sight to important elements for any seated or standing user."
- "It makes reaching to all components comfortable for any seated or standing user."
- "It accommodates variations in hand and grip size."
- "It provides adequate space for the use of assistive devices or personal assistance."

Principle seven is most likely the first principle which comes to mind when thinking about redesigning your home. Size and space appropriateness are major factors in augmenting your home for future growth. With this principle, your home will become a haven for your future lifestyle. Appropriate size and space for maneuverability relieve many of the risks associated with evolving in your own home. Stress is reduced with less chaos and clutter in the way of your activities of daily living.

Integrating Universal Design and the Americans with Disabilities Act Accessibility Guidelines

Many people are familiar with the existence of the Americans with Disabilities Act (ADA) of 1990 and the fact there are legal requirements for public accessibility. Though not legally required in a private residence, the ADA accessibility guidelines can offer recommended measurements you can use in your own home. They will give you a good start for evaluating your plan and provide you with specific ideas that best suit your personal needs.

Most commercial professional contractors are well versed in these guidelines. However, private contractors may not be. Seek contractors with proven experience in ADA requirements so they can tailor these to your home. Investigate the quality building projects in your area and contact their managers. Entire communities exist based on ADA guidelines and universal design.

Enlist designers who have proven experience in this area. Neighbors and friends are the best resource for referrals. Online resources such as Angie's List, Home Advisor, and Yelp are also helpful. Thoroughly consider your budget and obtain multiple bids. Since you are creating your own home for future growth, these regulations need to be used only as guidelines for implementing these principles. In each section below, I have included the precise dimensions recommended per ADA guidelines so you can begin to take measurements and see where you may need to make changes in your home.

Reality in Action

When I was a visiting nurse in an urban setting (before the use of GPS), I often needed to count the streets on a paper map and guess at the address to which I was being sent. The winter weather in New England caused the street signs to freeze and fall off throughout the season. It was also typical to find no numbers on houses or any sign that someone even lived there.

One day, as I counted four streets in and six houses beyond the main road, I thought I had found the house I was to visit. It was my first time at this man's home. My admission papers stated he was hard of hearing, so I knocked at the front door and there was no answer. I then went to the back door. A few minutes later, I heard a rustling of pans. A small woman came to the door wielding a large knife and screaming fearfully in a foreign language. I ran, *fast*. I was, indeed, at the wrong house. Needless to say, my patient did not get a prompt nursing visit that day. This brings me to the importance of entrances.

Entrances

I added this story to prove a point about signage and safety. Is your home visible and identifiable enough for you to obtain help if necessary? Visual access will keep the bad guys out and let the helpful people in. Global positioning satellite maps help today but are still not foolproof. Consider adding large address numbers to your home in view of the street and trimming hedges and trees that may be obscuring the view of your home.

Visual access is also important for your own safety for getting in and out of your home. You can never have enough lighting. For example, you may have difficulty with the entry door or finding the keyhole. Lighting and visibility are small, inexpensive changes which add ease for yourself in accessing your home and can also be helpful to other people entering your home.

Physical access is the next barrier to evaluate. When you enter your home, are there difficulties with steps, doors, handles, or fall risks? I really do not consider weather very much in Arizona, but when I lived in New England, it was a prime physical barrier for most homes.

Is your entryway wet or frozen much of the year? Are there rocks or debris? Are your pets waiting anxiously to trip you up? Railings and ramps may be needed in entry areas. Also consider the increased space that may be needed for equipment in the future.

ADA Guidelines for Entrances

The ADA offers guidelines for the minimum clearance and width of doorways to allow access for people with a variety of disabilities and access requirements. Section 4.13.5 of the ADA Standards for Accessible Design Revision of July 1, 1994, states, "Doorways shall have a minimum clear opening of 32 inches (815 mm) with the door open 90 degrees, measured between the face of the door and the opposite stop. Openings more than 24 inches (610 mm) in depth shall comply with 4.2.1 and 4.3.3" (*Code of Federal Regulations*, 2010).

Wheelchairs and Space

Wheelchairs are another consideration when it comes to preparing your home for your future needs. While you may not need one permanently, you may need one temporarily upon your return from the hospital.

The ADA outlines the space needed and reach ranges for wheelchair use in section "4.2 Space Allowance and Reach Ranges." According to the ADA, "The minimum clear width for single wheelchair passage shall be 32 inches (815 mm) at a point and 36 inches (915 mm) continuously" (*Code of Federal Regulations*, 2010).

This section also outlines the turning space required for wheelchair accessibility. It states, "The space required for a wheelchair to make an 18-degree turn is a clear space of 60 inches (1525 mm) or a T-shaped space" (*Code of Federal Regulations*, 2010).

Section 4.2.4.1 details size and approach for wheelchairs. "The minimum clear floor or ground space required to accommodate a single, stationary wheelchair and occupant is 30 inches by 48 inches (760 mm by 1220 mm). The minimum clear floor or ground space for wheelchairs may be positioned for forward or parallel approach to an object. Clear floor or ground space for wheelchairs may be part of the knee space under some objects" (*Code of Federal Regulations*, 2010).

Ramps

Wheelchairs also require ramps for entry. Think about your home. Are there stairs leading up to it from the sidewalk or driveway? Is there a big step at the threshold of the door? Consider how someone in a wheelchair, such as you arriving home from the hospital, could achieve entry.

The ADA also outlines what constitutes a ramp as well as ramp accessibility. Section 4.8.1 requires, "Any part of an accessible route with a slope greater than 1:20 shall be considered a ramp and shall comply with 4.8" (*Code of Federal Regulations*, 2010). Section 4.8.2 addresses the "Slope and Rise" of ramps. "The least possible slope shall be used for any ramp. The maximum slope of a ramp in new construction shall be 1:12. The maximum rise for any run shall be 30 inches (760 mm). Curb ramps and ramps to be constructed on existing sites or in existing buildings or facilities may have slopes and rises allowed in 4.1.6 if space limitations prohibit the use of 1:12 slope or less." The clear width of ramps, according to section 4.8.3, shall have a minimum clear width of 36 inches (915 mm) (*Code of Federal Regulations*, 2010).

Please note that these are just a few of the ADA regulations that can apply to a new home or remodel. You will want to review the

ADA guidelines for yourself and work with someone who is familiar with them when preparing your home for future accessibility.

Depending on the materials and style chosen, modifications for wheelchair accessibility including ramps can run into the thousands of dollars. Such modifications can cost from about $1,000 to $4,000, according to HomeAdvisor, which tracks home repair prices nationwide (1999-2019).

Planning for Emergency Access

I believe it is necessary to plan for someone to have emergency access to your home. Not only will this benefit you when you are unable to tend to it, but it can save your life in the event of a medical emergency. Think about adding a key box and an alarm system to your home, especially if you live alone.

In chapter two, I spoke about getting to know your neighbors. Introverts may find this idea to be against their general temperament. But simply being aware of your neighbors' presence and routines adds to your safety. Your neighbors provide support systems which cannot be replicated at any other home.

There are neighborhood watch programs, HOA groups, and applications which limits communication to between neighbors only. They may be doing the same projects and can exchange goods and services to create your lifelong dream homes together. Also, I suggest working with certified architects and construction companies that are familiar with ADA requirements. You can find a list of architects and construction companies on the ADA National Network (adata.org) under architects and contractors or through the National Association of Home Builders (nahb.org).

If you are assisting someone with planning for a future in their home, you may ask, "How long can mom and dad live in their own home? What happens if they cannot stay there?" If you have given someone this book as a gift to assist them in later life, chances are you are concerned about them. Performing these pieces of the home assessment as a group activity can help alleviate your concerns. The reason for this is that you have become proactive in creating a safer environment by investing in your home or the home of your loved one.

Fall Prevention

Preventing falls is of primary importance for home safety. This is true especially after hospitalization. From past experience as a home care nurse, I have learned that throw rugs and unsteady furniture are accidents waiting to happen. I have found that patients have a certain denial about using canes and walkers when they were previously comfortable at home without them. As a result, they tend to lean on the furniture and are hesitant to move tripping hazards like rugs. Uneven floors and thresholds also pose a tripping hazard and are often overlooked. Even my own mother was resistant to use her cane while she was in the house despite her unsteadiness.

Furniture and countertops are not grab bars. Neither are doorways and toilet paper holders. Denial is one of the reasons that many people are not proactively preparing their environments for easy living.

As I had stated previously, there is no reason to demolish the character of your home even if your passageways are not wide enough. There are many options available to widen doorways without demolition. Two such available strategies include different types of doors and hinges. If you wanted to replace the door, a pocket door or a barn door could give you approximately two extra inches of clearance. If you wanted to replace only the hinges, there are three-piece hinges available which tuck the door behind the entrance which also give another one to two inches of extra clearance. If your house is truly inaccessible, consider hiring a contractor who specializes in universal home design. These contractors are very adept at reconfiguring spaces for maneuverability.

Modifying Rooms in Your Home and ADA Guidelines

Now that you have accessed the rooms in your home, the next section deals with recommendations for making various rooms more accessible to everyone. Not only do I make recommendations based on my own experiences and observations as a home care nurse, but I have included information from ADA guidelines that may give you some additional help in planning for your future at home.

Bathrooms

Let's begin with the all-important bathroom. The ideal bathroom would be located on the same level as the master bedroom. If your home is set up differently from this, now is the time to reconsider a major renovation. Most falls and accidents occur in bathrooms, so this is the primary target of most renovations to increase ease-of-use and safety.

While floundering through my own home in my post hospital uniform, I found difficulty in grasping items of daily use, especially in the sink and shower. These are areas where touch sensitive handles and faucets may be useful. Handheld shower nozzles on vertical sliders and shower seats will make life easier. Consider also preset temperatures for your water to prevent burns. Think about your specific needs and design your bathroom to fit your lifestyle.

Consider a total master plan before starting any remodeling or renovation in your bathroom. Assess the main necessities in your current bathroom. As you did in the other rooms, use all your senses to spot barriers. Did you notice enough space for maneuverability? Were the sinks and toilets an appropriate height for easy reachability? Were there slipping and/or tripping hazards? Always take into consideration the favorable qualities which already exist in your bathroom. Include these in your master plan for renovation or remodeling as well.

Since most of your activities of daily living primarily focus around the bathroom, it is imperative to focus on this area intensely. Spend as much time as possible in your assessment. You may need to do this over several days and under different circumstances. Consider the quality of your fixtures. Also consider the stability and durability of the equipment. In the bathroom, many people use the furnishings to provide stability as they maneuver around.

The ideal situation would be to have enough space for maneuverability of a walker or wheelchair. Additional space for a caregiver to access you in any room would be an added bonus. If there is not adequate space for these items, consider space for maneuverability in your master plan for remodeling or renovations.

Section 4.24.5 of the ADA Guidelines, for example, gives direction for space needed for accessibility to sinks including those in wheelchairs. "A clear floor space at least 30 inches by 48 inches (760 mm by 1220 mm) complying with 4.2.4 shall be provided in front of a sink to allow forward approach. The clear floor space shall be on an accessible route and shall extend a maximum of 19 inches (485 mm) underneath the sink" (*Code of Federal Regulations*, 2010).

There are also hundreds of resources such as access-board.gov to help you if you are having difficulty assessing the needs in your bathroom. Medicare, for example, will cover an occupational therapy assessment with a prescription from your doctor. These resources can be found through the American Occupational

Therapy Association at AOTA.org. A professional assessment, in addition with your own personal assessment of your environment, will ensure that you have the best chance of success.

Your individual assessment will lead you to analyze your specialized needs. For example, take into consideration the medical conditions that you already have. What do you anticipate your needs will be based on these conditions?

In my own situation, when I visited my primary care physician, I complained about having gained a few pounds. As I was getting older, I neglected to realize my metabolism was not keeping up with my caloric intake. My primary care physician jokingly asked me, "Can you run as fast as you did 20 years ago?" When I responded with "No," he then asked, "Then why do you expect your body to run as fast as it did 20 years ago?"

It was funny that I had not given this any thought previously, but denial was a strong factor in my avoiding preparation for the future. Somehow, I expected my health to never decline and my body to continue functioning at an optimal level. Unfortunately, I realized this was not to be the case and, inevitably, I would have to make some adjustments. Hopefully, widening the bathroom door just for my own body to fit through would not be one of those adjustments; but, widening the bathroom door for equipment seemed acceptable to me.

To improve the flow of maneuverability to the main items in your bathroom, swing-away and trifold hinges can add approximately two inches to your entrances. As previously mentioned, barn doors and pocket doors are other options. For less than $100 in materials cost, you can replace the door with a larger one and doorjambs (Khalfani-Cox, 2017). Remove steps, thresholds, and rugs that increase the risk of falls.

The shower, toilet, sink, and tub should be accessible. To increase accessibility in this area, consider new fixtures. Keep in mind your personal preferences and your personal needs. Think about your personal style and use your creativity to combine ease-of-use and the beauty of your environment.

Sinks

When entering your bathroom and encountering your ADLs, the first thing you are likely to notice is the sink. You need to be able to reach it sitting in a wheelchair or standing with a walker or cane so you can wash your hands, brush your teeth, or clean your face. There are several ADA recommendations to make the sink universally accommodating in your home.

Section 4.24.2 outlines that sinks should be mounted with the counter or rim being no higher than 34 inches (865 mm) above the finish floor. This is important for knee clearance which is outlined in section 4.24.3 of the ADA guidelines. "Knee clearance that is at least 27 inches (685 mm) high, 30 inches (760 mm) wide, and 19 inches (485 mm) deep shall be provided underneath sinks" (*Code of Federal Regulations*, 2010).

Sinks should be a maximum depth of 6.5 inches (165 mm) deep (section 4.24.2) and faucets should be "lever-operated, push-type, touch-type, or electronically controlled mechanisms" to make them easily accessible, according to section 4.24.7. You'll also need to consider exposed pipes and surfaces under the sink, which should be "insulated or otherwise configured so as to protect against contact." To avoid injury, there should also be nothing sharp or abrasive under the sink surfaces (*Code of Federal Regulations*, 2010).

Shower

Because the shower involves running water, it is a place where many falls occur. There are things you can do to reduce your risk or the risk of others for falls. The ADA recommends in section 4.21.6 that the shower include a spray hose that is at least 60 inches (1525 mm) long that can be used both as a fixed showerhead and as a hand-held shower. The ADA also requires grab bars, ample clear floor space, and that shower stalls be 36 inches by 36 inches (915 mm by 915 mm) in size. Additionally, if a seat is needed, the ADA provides guidelines for shower seats as well (*Code of Federal Regulations*, 2010).

Bathtubs

While showers are ideal in some situations, many people like to relax in a bathtub and some conditions require it for treatment. You can remodel your bathroom to include a walk-in tub if your current bathtub doesn't offer ease of access though these can put a dent in your remodeling budget.

"Shower and bath combination stalls may require a lot of time and effort for installation. They can also cost upward of $1,000" (Khalfani-Cox, 2017).

The ADA recommends clearing floor space in front of bathtubs and in-tub seats can make bathing easier. Seats should be mounted securely and should not slip during use as outlined in section 4.20.3 of the ADA guidelines (*Code of Federal Regulations*, 2010).

The Toilet or Water Closet

As a nurse I have seen many needs in the toilet area. Toilet risers and secure handrails will most likely be needed. Be creative and consider comfort items such as padded and heated seats, bidets, and night lighting. As you research the new possibilities and bathroom remodeling you may be surprised at all the features you can include to make your bathroom welcoming and safe.

For starters, make sure the height of your toilet is 17 inches to 19 inches (430 mm to 485 mm) as measured to the top of the toilet seat from the floor. Flush controls can be hand operated or automatic. Whatever control you prefer should be mounted on the wide side of the toilet area no more than 44 inches (1120 mm) above the floor, according to ADA guidelines (*Code of Federal Regulations*, 2010).

Grab bars can be installed discreetly for safety while keeping the beautiful integrity of your design. Just as in the shower or bathtub, grab bars can help people to maneuver more easily. Section 4.16.4 of the ADA guidelines require that grab bars behind the water closet be 36 inches (915 mm) minimum (*Code of Federal Regulations*, 2010).

Stable, nonskid flooring can also be aesthetically pleasing as well. There are many flooring choices available which provide beauty and a reliable, safe texture. For example, occupational therapists advise the use of nonskid strips instead of mats in the bathtub and shower to avoid toe edges.

Be sure to enjoy the process of remodeling to make your bathroom your personal sanctuary. Since the bathroom is an area which needs an overall master plan, incorporate all of these elements into your design. Focus on safety and ease of use. Consider form and function.

My mantra throughout this process became, "Something is better than nothing." I felt such a sense of accomplishment when I installed *one* grab bar in my shower. I knew I was on the way to an equipped home. Start small and relish in your successes, even the small ones.

Bedrooms

Let's move on to the bedrooms. Restful sleep is a prime concern especially after hospitalization. Much recovery occurs during sleep. Nothing is as gratifying and rejuvenating as a good night's sleep. Again, pay special attention to your personal style and your safety needs.

The location of your bedroom, whether it be on the first or second floor, can pose an issue. A bedroom on the first floor may not be the master bedroom and, therefore, may not have ensuite facilities. A bedroom on the second floor obviously poses a problem of continual accessibility. There are many things you can do in these situations. It depends on your budget and to what extreme you would like to renovate. Some options I have seen are chair elevators, lift elevators, and sturdy handrails.

Another overall consideration for your home is to repurpose the functions of your existing rooms. A den, a study, or any other large room can be converted into a master bedroom with an ensuite or bathroom nearby. A first-floor bedroom is a precious asset. Think creatively about the current flow of your home. Reconfiguring rooms or an entire section of your home may be necessary for universal design.

As you moved your bedroom during your assessment did you check all areas to suit your needs? For example, did you consider the height of electrical outlets, the sturdiness of the structures and furniture, and the area surrounding your bed? Evaluate this room and other rooms for the need for smoke detectors and carbon dioxide (CO_2) detectors. When you tried to open and close the windows and doors, was it difficult? As always, focus on varying levels of lighting depending on your activities in the bedroom.

Bedroom Furnishings

Some adjustments in furniture may be necessary as well. Lifting recliners and adjustable beds with remote controls can ease your efforts of movement. There should be adequate space around your bed for maneuverability as well. Consider remote controls in the areas of lighting, temperature, and the use of entertainment equipment.

Tailor your bedroom to be as luxurious as possible regarding these items and other amenities for your enjoyment. Be mindful of restful colors, degrees of lighting, and scents which you prefer. Visualize your ideal bedroom. An accessible, safe room need not be devoid of beauty and comfort.

Storage

Another primary need in the bedroom is storage. As you practiced in full costume and attempted to dress yourself in your current bedroom, was it difficult accessing your clothing? This activity will shed light on your needs for accessible storage.

Also, consider your most used items and their location. Store a cache of loose clothing for easy dressing after a hospitalization. In reference to closets, drawers, and shelves, rollouts and roll-unders bring items to within your reachability. As you would in any other room, explore what is available in newly remodeled homes. You may want to visit some active adult communities for ideas as well. One particularly good site is Lennar.com.

The Laundry Room

As you walked through your bedroom, you undoubtedly realized the need for a laundry nearby. Laundry rooms should be close enough to transfer your clothes back and forth but far enough so that you don't have to deal with the noise of the washer and dryer.

Most adaptable homes have front loading washers and dryers. Both are raised about one to two feet off the ground for easier loading. Dispensers for soaps and other laundry products should be clearly labeled and easy to access. Water temperatures for each load can also be preset to avoid burns.

Kitchens

As you continue through your home, the next area of most importance will be the kitchen. As a visiting nurse, I have seen kitchens in every shape, size, and function. I have seen them on the first floor and the second floor. The barriers can be numerous especially because we spend so much time in our kitchen. Think of the things that we do there. We prepare food. We socialize. We gather with our families there. The kitchen is the hub of the home and a very important place to have safe and organized.

Some things to consider in your kitchen are reachability and organization. All your basic appliances and cooking utensils probably reside here. Think about when you were going through your kitchen with the gloves on. Was it difficult to open drawers and cabinets? Were you able to reach microwaves and dishwashers? Was the height of items appropriate for perhaps a wheelchair? Or were you stuck and unable to get through a small entranceway to even access the kitchen?

ADA Guidelines in the Kitchen

There are things you will need to consider in the kitchen to make it more universally accessible for everyone. The kitchen offers many obstacles in most homes because it is the busiest place. I would first suggest clearing away the obstacles on the floor.

Cleanliness is also very important in the kitchen since food preparation will occur there. Are your cleaning products accessible? Do you have a plan that's laid out in case someone else needs to do your cleaning for a while? Are there any particular methods that you prefer to be used on your countertops and sinks? The floors also need to be considered for cleanliness and freedom from clutter to prevent falls.

I would suggest a written plan for cleaning and organizing your kitchen with a list of products you would like to use on each surface. Organize the kitchen with labels to establish a home for all your items. With labels hidden inside of drawers and doors aesthetics need not be compromised. Remember, ease-of-use and the integrity of your home are priorities.

This is especially important if you need to hire assistance for your meal preparation. These services are generally paid for on an hourly basis and their time is valuable. Think of yourself as if it were the time you came home from a hospital. After you settle in, you likely will want a meal. Ask yourself how easy it would be for someone to prepare you a meal in your kitchen. Where are the pots and pans? Are the glasses and silverware in a place that makes sense to a person who is unfamiliar with your kitchen? Is your food pantry orderly? The ultimate success here is for a person who is unfamiliar with your kitchen to be able to quickly and easily prepare your meal without delay and frustration.

In the future, when you are preparing your own meals, take into consideration reach ability and the organization of your kitchen. Take hints from residences that have been designed as handicapped accessible. I have visited many senior housing developments as a nurse. Most of the kitchens in these residences have relocated frequently used items. For instance, dishwashers are appearing as drawers because they can pull out and be easily filled without bending. Microwaves are often placed on countertops instead of over the stove (Wingler, 2014).

"Ideally you would measure individual comfort ranges for working in the kitchen for whom the kitchen is being accommodated" (Wingler, 2014). Consider also countertops, cabinets, appliances, and sinks for barriers and potential hazards.

Section 4.32.4 of the ADA Guidelines addresses the height of tables or counters.

The guidelines state, "The tops of accessible tables and counters shall be from 28 inches to 34 inches (710 mm to 865 mm) above the floor finish or ground." You'll also need to consider knee clearances under counters and tables for people in wheelchairs which is addressed in Section 4.32.3. "If seating for people in wheelchairs is provided at tables or counters, knee spaces at least 27 inches (685 mm) high, 30 inches (760 mm) wide, and 19 inches (485 mm) deep shall be provided" (*Code of Federal Regulations*, 2010).

Depending on the extent of your preparation, the possibilities are endless. Build using various heights needed whether you are in a wheelchair or are using a walker or cane. Roll under sinks and roll out appliances can be installed. Lowering electrical outlets and light fixtures are other common upgrades. I have even seen elevators added to homes to make use of every level. The point of this exercise is to think creatively and weigh the risks and benefits of your remodeling.

Storage

Storage is another issue in the kitchen that is always contentious. According to Janis Kent's blog in *Stepping Thru Accessibility* online, "ADA Requirements for Kitchen Storage," upper shelves can actually be removed from wall cabinets to reduce the inaccessible portion of kitchen storage (2015).

Adding an island with extra storage underneath can be easily done in most kitchens. Extra roll out drawers in cabinets are handy to bring items to you. As I have remodeled my own kitchen, I have discovered that planning and designing the kitchen completely in one process is most efficient. Piecing items together will make remodeling more complicated.

When adding major items to your kitchen like cabinets, appliances, islands, and countertops, it is best to start with a full plan. This will make it easier to stay on budget, as well. Seek qualified ADA contractors via referral or visit the ADA National Network online for recommended architects and contractors.

Consider the details in your plan. As you moved through your house with your gloves, did you notice the handles? Handles on sinks, cabinets, and drawers can easily be replaced with levers or touch control centers. Grab bars can also be added near sinks and stoves discreetly for maneuvering around your kitchen. "Replacing doorknobs with a lever door handle — for around $20 to $25 — is a low-cost solution" (Khalfani-Cox, 2017).

Living Rooms

Moving on to the main living area of your home, consider the size of the area needed to skillfully maneuver, perhaps in a wheelchair or with a walker. Arrange furniture against walls or in the manner that leaves clearance for transfers. Repurpose empty corners to push furniture for maximum floor space. Leave a circular area of about 30 to 48 inches around your favorite seating area.

During my research, I have found many user-friendly items. For instance, self-lifting recliners, remote-controlled entertainment systems, and skylights are all helpful. Consider a measured blueprint before moving furniture. Design your living room thoroughly and try to maintain the same set up to establish familiarity.

Cluttered floors and tripping hazards are especially important to avoid in your living area. Remove area rugs and extraneous decorative items from the floor. Rather than tossing them out, consider hanging sentimental and decorative items on your walls.

After decluttering my own home, I found it to be a very liberating experience leaving increased space and less maintenance. A surprise bonus was the relief of emotional clutter as well. One of the best books I have found on the subject is *The Life-Changing Magic of Tidying Up: The Japanese Art of Decluttering and Organizing* by Marie Kondo. See the resources page at the end of this book for additional resources and helpful information.

To make the floor safer in your living room and beyond, consider small, affordable changes you can make. Khalfani-Cox made several recommendations in her article.

"A number of materials provide traction and cushion, including nonslip vinyl, rubber flooring, and cork, which is typically less than $3 per square foot. Cheaper solutions, such as slip-resistant rugs for around $10 to $15 apiece, may be more cost effective for those on a budget. Nonslip bathmats with suction cups for only $10 or so, nonslip sprays that typically run $20 to $30, and water-resistant adhesives that cost about $40 to $50" (Khalfani-Cox, 2017).

Lighting

As you moved through your home with your glasses did you notice the areas of dim light? Natural light is highly valued when someone is evaluating a home. However, natural light is not always possible in every area of your home.

There are many new light sources available which have been developed to include in homes. Some examples are skylights, solar tubes, and motion-sensor or touch-sensor lighting. A beautiful way to add your personal touch and safety to your home is to properly install high-quality lighting.

Knowing Your Home

The beauty of your home renovation project is three-fold. First, it's your home, your rules. Next, your renovation allows for growth in your forever home in everything from accessibility to learning about your home. Finally, it embellishes your love for your personal space on your journey to enjoying a lifetime in your own home.

As you have experienced this journey of discovery in your own home, you have likely learned more about all the resources it has to offer. This is good as you should be aware of all your resource lines in your home such as control valves for your water, gas, and electric shutoffs. Everything should be clearly labeled so that if you needed help you, a friend, or contractor could easily remedy the problem. As in the other areas of your home, the goal is ease-of-use, reachability, and maneuverability.

In conclusion, safety and security provide comfort and well-being at home. When thinking about aging in place, long-term safety is key. Factors include your physical and visual access, safety from falls, and access to neighbors. For additional ideas for making your home safe, effortless, beautiful, and universally accessible, you can research design ideas online.

4

FINANCIAL PLANNING &
SUSTAINABLE INCOME

"You can't eat your rugs, honey."
~Anna, a former patient

As you read through the previous chapters including "A Typical Hospital Experience," you were undoubtedly flooded with financial questions. How would I afford an unexpected hospital stay? Would all my investments and resources be drained? What does my insurance cover? Should continually paying for health insurance negate all of my personal costs?

Chapter 3 probably left you with another set of financial

questions. Will remodeling my home and planning for my future reap enough benefits to make it a worthwhile investment? Does it need to cost so much? The answers to these questions vary for each individual.

Your decision to enjoy a lifetime in your own home weighs heavily on your needs, your determination, and your financial resources. Financial planning is something every one must think about as their working years decrease and their financial needs increase. Whether you are retired or are still working, there are many ways to adapt to the changing financial climate of your household.

Focus on Value

I was recently speaking to Luis, an electrical inspector, and I told him I was looking for someone to interview for this book. He was very excited to tell me about his mother who was 92 years old and lived alone in their childhood home. He stated that it was a very small home on one level that had not changed since he could remember.

Luis said he was the youngest of 14 children and that their family was very close. Every weekend one of the 14 children spent the day with their mother to check on her and help with her errands. Luis said his mother was very old-fashioned, set in her ways, and she knew the value of investing in herself.

She and her husband had such a large family and lived through such hard times that she knew how to live below her means. In order to live below her means, she was a master of the basic necessities. She was a master cook, could repair anything, and she knew how to barter for a good deal. Her values persisted through her entire life and her determination to live on her own reflected this.

From week to week she followed the same routine. Saving, investing, learning, and do-it-yourself projects were natural to her. When her children came to visit, they usually found her happily following her routine. It seems that Luis' mother had built an enriched life by investing in herself and her family.

This woman was very mindful of her basic needs. Her years of experience in raising a family on a limited budget forced her to build a skill set as an asset greater than any investment. She was very aware of the value of things and she was very aware of the value of her abilities. Her expertise and independent do-it-yourself attitude protected her family from draining their hard-earned savings.

Anna

In an extreme contrast to Luis' mother, Anna lived a life of luxury. As her visiting nurse, I found I lacked empathy for her until I heard her strange story. Anna was a tiny, feisty woman who lived alone following the death of her husband.

It was 1984 and Anna was living in an elegant townhome in a more prestigious area of the same city. She was struggling. Anna wanted to remain in her rented space, but her previous unrestrained lifestyle had left her unable to afford her current needs. She was too feeble to meet me outside when I first arrived. I rang the buzzer to be let into her home.

A vast townhome with lavish Victorian draperies and wall to wall carpeting surrounded Anna. Gold tones, modern in her era, were signs of wealth. Her detailed, small profile was lit by the reflection of extravagant chandeliers. There was nothing that suggested hardship.

Visiting her as a nurse seemed almost unnecessary as I had assumed she could have afforded a private, full-time caregiver. I was there to assess her congestive heart failure symptoms, teach her management of her chronic condition, and evaluate her for fluid overload. Nursing visits in 1984 was a cost-effective means of keeping chronic patients out of the hospital and this program was very successful. Also, sneaking a glimpse of day-to-day life for a dependent, chronically-ill person enabled me to make an educated guess about her future.

In this case, I suspected Anna would remain happily in her home for a lifetime. I was wrong. As I assessed Anna's diet, she informed me that she had not eaten that day and was relying on "TV dinners" for sustenance. This translated to frozen aluminum foil-covered-convenience meals laden with heavy salt. Salt is the number one enemy of anyone with congestive heart failure. Nutritional counseling became my highest priority for this visit.

You might find yourself wondering why this woman was eating this way. The answer is that she was alone in the world with no one to cook for her. She was not strong enough to manage preparing a large meal in an oven. She had no transportation. Her income was limited and she was still paying rent.

Why hadn't I seen this immediately? I had initially failed to look beyond the cover of her life's book and I neglected the content of her lifestyle. She was, in today's terms, "cash poor." Unwittingly enough, she was also poor socially and in spirit. Since she qualified, I was able to set up Meals on Wheels for her.

As I left my first appointment with her, Anna said to me bluntly, *"You can't eat your rugs, honey."*

This phrase changed my approach to enjoying a lifetime in my own home. It has resonated in me for more than 30 years. Her short quip redefined success in life. Anna's comment was like a smack in the face. It demonstrated the importance of focusing on relationships, financial freedom, and prioritizing for your future. I still joke with my husband about it. Anna had cut to the chase and I still appreciate her advice.

In a snapshot of your typical week, how much time do you spend on things of value? You may want to jot down a week's worth of your activities. Break down this list into the needed routine items, activities, and services which bring joy to your life. Weed out the non-essentials. Cut out the clutter of the mundane. This process leads to delight in your future forever home.

Improving Your Financial Health

There are several essential, basic steps you should take in order to improve your financial health to ensure a lifetime of aging in place in the comfort of your own home. Begin with these three simple steps toward financial health: Save, build wealth, and extend your income for future sustainability.

Step One: Save

The first step to saving money is to being tracking your day-to-day expenses. You'll find that most budgets begin with tracking expenses in *real time*. Set aside a specific time and diligently track all of you expenditures.

In addition, examine prior checkbooks and credit card statements. One to three months' worth of statements should give you an overall view of your spending. For example, follow your next month's purchases and record them. Then, add the past two months of records of account transactions for an unbiased *real time* list. Do not skip this process.

An accurate budget depends on your specific needs and realistic, real-time purchases. The goal is to have extra money at the end of the pay period to build an emergency fund. An emergency fund should be easily accessible cash in accounts to be used for expenses that cannot wait. The amount in this fund should be based upon a percentage of your total investments taking into consideration your age and your health.

According to an article by Paula Pant, "The 50/30/20 Rule of Thumb for Budgeting," at least 20 percent of your income should go towards your savings. Another 50 percent (maximum) should go toward your necessities. The remaining 30 percent should then go toward discretionary items (Pant, 2019). This is called the 50/30/20 rule and it is becoming popular quick-and-easy financial advice.

"It's the '20' in the 50/30/20 rule," Pant wrote. "It's in a class all its own. You should spend at least 20 percent of your after-tax income repaying debts, saving money in your emergency fund, and your retirement accounts. If you carry a credit card balance, the minimum payment is a 'need' and it counts toward the 50 percent" (Pant, 2019).

Saving money results in incrementally building wealth. Make your money work as hard as you do. I have found that a great preliminary use of this newfound way to saving is to streamline it into one institution. This has a twofold benefit.

First, as you enjoy aging in your own home, you will need help along the way. Having your assets in one place makes it easier for yourself and anyone who may need to assist you in the future. By having your assets in one place, it allows your banker and/or financial advisor a simple snapshot of what you have to work with so they can offer you the best financial advice possible.

Secondly, there are many perks offered by combining your banking and investing institutions. These perks may include free checking, free ATM use, free safe deposit boxes, and more importantly, freedom from minimum balances. Discounted financial advisement services are also a possibility if your assets are substantial.

A financial advisor will advise you about investing your funds with a proper distribution of risk based on your age and income level. In contrast, a financial manager will have access to your funds and be able to make decisions on your behalf. Financial advisors may not even charge you at all if you have substantial assets in the bank. Financial managers typically charge a percentage of managed assets or flat fees for their administrative efforts. Check with your financial advisor or financial manager to find out their rates.

Creating a Plan & Actuality

Based on your real-time spending, create a written budget. For example, there are handwritten types, cash systems with envelopes, or computer spreadsheets. Unlimited apps and programs exist to write your budget. Choose the easiest system suited to your needs to increase your long-term success.

This process is a slow steady one. Once you have a written budget of your basic needs, it will be much easier to live below your means. You can find templates online such as those available at www.smartsheet.com. There you can determine which budget template best matches your needs and use it in developing a realistic budget.

When creating a budget, you need to ask yourself several questions. Does your budget reflect your basic needs? Look back to your real-time purchases. These basic needs should be a predetermined part of your budget. These are fixed expenses that you can predict with adequate reliability each month.

Beyond the fixed expenses, examine the things which are

valuable to you and require part of your monthly budget. Eliminate the things that are extravagant and use that money to build an emergency fund. Plan for the unexpected. Unexpected expenses happen randomly and without warning but they always happen. Saving and living below your means will eventually free you from indebtedness and enrich your life.

Basically, any service that you can provide for yourself or any item that you can obtain without a purchase saves you double in taxes. Really consider what you need for your daily living and to enrich your life in the future. Rather than spending money on something unnecessary now that won't enrich your life later, you can save those funds for something you may need later on.

By investing part of your pretax income into your 401K or other retirement plan, you will avoid immediately paying income tax on those funds. Instead of using those funds now to make a purchase, you can defer the income tax on that money that you earned simply by saving it. You'll also save on the sales tax which you would pay on the item as well. Do-it-yourself, make-it-yourself, and invest in yourself. You'll save double on taxes. Your penalties will also be reduced by not accumulating debt.

The next area of the budget refers to variable expenses. A variable expense is an expense that you know is coming but can't necessarily plan for. Variable expenses can include unexpected emergencies, vacations, maintenance of homes and cars, medical expenses, gifts, and any other expense which does not come on a regular basis. This will be the majority of your budget. At the end of the chapter there will be many resources to help you create your written budget. The most important part is that you follow through in keeping to your budget by setting up the way you pay for things.

Personally, I prefer to use a credit card for most of my expenses. I gain a cash back reward with all purchases and I consolidate everything into one card. This keeps me from overspending due to having only one credit card. I pay the entire balance every month and, at the end of the month, I reconcile my budget with my actual spending. It is easily divided into categories by the credit card statement. If you are unable to track your expenses, a written budget will not be very useful to you.

Avoiding Debt

A primary way to invest in yourself is to *live below your means*. This may be something that you have been doing already or this may be a new concept to you. Know that indebtedness is a triple threat. It gives you a negative perception of yourself. It constantly adds to itself causing more indebtedness (i.e. interest). Lastly, it creates constant stress due to the loss of control of your future financial success.

The last resort in any emergency is to dip into investment funds, your 401(k), or any other resource which may involve a penalty. Having a good amount of liquid assets and/or readily available cash are key in an emergency. It should not be necessary to pay extra penalties or taxes to take out money which you have earned. Luckily, in his case, Angelo was able to draw on his emergency fund to acquire the basic equipment needed for Marie.

Step Two: Build Wealth

Investing, in itself, has proven a book-worthy subject. However, the basics are the same. A financial advisor can educate you about index funds, mutual fund, and stocks. For the sake of this limited section, I will focus on the most common investments.

Consider your largest investment. Your home is most likely one of your greatest assets. Since you are preparing for many gratifying years in your home, reflect on its ongoing and preventative costs. For example, maintenance of your larger investment is critical to maximize your home as an asset and as your absolute destination.

Just as you would for a car, create a maintenance schedule for your home. Get things fixed properly. Consider the value of your time when you retire versus the cost of projects. Decide which projects you would like to tackle based on your skills. By maintaining your home in advance, it will boost the value of your home and lessen stress when you have a crisis.

As you took an assessment of your home for remodeling, did you notice any repairs that your home needed? Had you considered any major appliances wearing down? Take time to do a fair appraisal of your home as if you were an inspector. Look at the protective elements such as: paint, roofing, air conditioning and heat, and water and sewer sources.

As technology progresses, you can make drastic changes to improve energy efficiency and savings. It is a good time to use your skills when you are remodeling your home. If you use outside help, save lists of maintenance professionals' names and numbers and the rating you gave them.

Evaluate all of the resources at your disposal. Even if your talents are not home related, they can be exchanged for the services of others. Have you ever heard of a painting party, yard work party, or a landscaping lunch? These parties are organized to exchange camaraderie, food, and fun for friends' and neighbors' assistance. Once you have a dedicated social circle, you can participate in this type of bartering. It is usually a fun event for all.

Streamline and Repeat

One of the things I noticed when speaking with people who have lived through hard times is their routine. Routine cuts through the unnecessary and focuses on things of value. It sets you on a path to streamline and repeat the elements in your life which you love the most. For example, if your routine is to cook at home then dining out becomes a special luxury. Or, the bonus of a long anticipated month-long vacation doubles in pleasure after a routine of shorter, more limited vacations.

The focus of living below your means is to streamline and repeat things of value. The determination of value is relevant to your personal style related to supply and demand. Basically, is the demand for your purchase in line with the supply of your resources? Is this service/ item a want or need? How much value do I place on a service/item in relation to the joy that it brings to me?

I value my free time. Thus, I set up mundane activities to be as easy as possible. No one delights in paying bills and tax planning. I have found that consolidating my purchases into one credit card and consolidating all of my accounts into one main bank has eased this chore. I have had experience with many families who lose track of their assets due to disorganization.

Along the same line of thinking, consolidating taxable versus nontaxable accounts makes it easier to strategize for the future. Your tax preparation will be less expensive when you come to your accountant with organized materials. Enjoying a lifetime in your own home will be more effortless without the concern of dealing with multiple banks and creditors. Streamline and repeat.

If you are still working, maximize your 401(k) or 403(b) account. Often employers will match these funds up to a certain percentage. This is your chance to diversify into stocks and bonds as investments. Be aware of the fees and other management charges in each fund. You will specifically find these in the funds' prospectus.

According to a piece in *Investopedia*, "A prospectus is a formal document that is required by and filed with the Securities and Exchange Commission (SEC) that provides details about an investment offering for sale to the public. A prospectus is filed for stock, bond, and mutual fund offerings. A prospectus is used to help investors make a more informed investment decision" (Chen & Murphy, 2019).

Carefully choose your investments in these accounts by consulting your financial advisor. You may find one at your workplace who is specifically educated about these funds. If there is not a financial advisor to speak with through your employer, you can also check with your bank or financial institution for one.

Step 3: Extend Income

According to the piece "The Power of Working Longer" by the *National Bureau of Economic Research*, "The basic result of working longer is that delaying retirement by three to six months has the same impact on the retirement standard of living as saving an additional one-percentage point of labor earnings for 30 years. The relative power of saving more is even lower if the decision to increase savings is made later in the work life" (Bronshtein, Scott, Shoven, & Slavov, 2018).

Working longer before retirement is gaining popularity. "The truth is, a lot of Americans simply can't afford to retire because they couldn't save enough during their working years. Conclusions on how well people are saving for retirement vary by financial institution or agency, but one analysis from U.S. Census Bureau researchers found about only a third of workers are saving in employer-sponsored accounts" (Malito, 2018).

Delaying retirement by working longer may or may not be an option for you. If you dread continuing with your full-time occupation, consider alternatives in addition to prolonging your present career. Part-time work is offered in some professions. However, if this is beyond your reach, consider a boost by means of a passive income.

"Passive income is earnings derived from a rental property, limited partnership, or other enterprise in which a person is not actively involved. As with active income, passive income is usually taxable" (Chen, 2019).

As you have learned, living below your means is of extreme importance. If you are older and concerned that you haven't saved enough for your future, there are many other avenues to establishing passive income. In addition to the other preparations in this book, this will take a deliberate investment, perhaps in time and money. It will increase your security and well being as you age in your own home.

There are an abundance of income streams in addition to the well-known areas of rental property and limited partnerships. These are commonly referred to as "side hustles." Side hustles can range from work-at-home activities to developing a personal hobby into a money-making business. Millennials seem to be the masters of the side hustle.

Side hustles can include small businesses which run themselves with minimal management. These types of businesses include laundromats, coin-operated vending machines, automatic car washes, and e-books. With any of these types of businesses there may be some initial expense; however, the long-term cash flow implications will provide an easy, sustainable, passive income. Look for types of businesses with low maintenance and a very limited or nonexistent staff.

Look to millennials for more up-to-date sources of passive income. They use technology in their favor. With sites such as YouTube, Pinterest, blogs, and vlogs, you can share any talent and earn money from advertising on your site. Consider the skills and interests you possess. For example, if photography is your passion, you can create stock photos and graphics templates for businesses. If marketing is your forte, use YouTube for your reviews and testimonials on your favorite products. If you have talent in teaching and a knack for reaching struggling students, you may consider offering online courses or private tutoring. As your prepare your home, sites like eBay and Shopify offer buy, sell, and trade capabilities if you are heavier on possessions and lighter on aptitude.

Deliberate planning of multiple sources of sustainable income will enrich your life and enable you to remain in your own home. These efforts are a great investment for you and your family when you consider the cost of the alternatives.

The online article "How Much Does Assisted Living and Home Care Cost in the US?" at Seniorliving.org outlines the high cost of assisted living in America. Assisted living communities and independent living communities generally have a monthly rate. These monthly costs range from "$2,537 in Missouri to $6,700 in Washington, D.C.," (2019).

These costs can be in addition to certain hospitality and care services available for a higher monthly fee. Some assisted living communities and independent living communities may require a move-in fee, which could equal one month's rent or less. To know your actual costs, you'll need to visit with a community sales counselor.

The piece "What Does it Cost?" from whereyoulivematters.org states, "A Life Plan Community (also known as a CCRC, or continuing care retirement community) usually has an entrance fee. It's the upfront cost most people handle with proceeds from selling their houses. Entrance fees range from around $100,000 upward, depending on floor plans and residential contracts, or the region where you reside. In addition, Life Plan Communities typically have monthly service fees, ranging from $1,000 to $5,000 or more. To know your actual costs, you'll need to visit with the community sales counselor" (2019).

According to the blog "What Does a Nursing Home Cost?" on *RetirementLiving.com*, "The cost of a nursing home varies significantly depending on the location. For example, in Alaska, the average cost for a private room is $800 per day, whereas the same room in Oklahoma would cost an average of $147 per day. Nursing homes in popular cities tend to cost more than in rural areas" (2019).

With masterful social networking (friends, family, support groups, etc.) and financial planning (passive income and investing), retaining your independent life at home will be more cost effective. The online article "The Cost of Aging in Place Remodeling" by *RetirementLiving.com*, "Aging in place costs less than the alternative. The good news is that price tag on most remodeling projects is under $10,000, which is still far less than what you might spend on a nursing home" (2019).

Future Sustainable Income

For this portion of the book, I had the great pleasure of interviewing a well-known, certified public accountant (CPA) with more than 35 years of experience, Ron Fuoco. Ron has an established career in public and private accounting with a specialty in cost accounting and national and international taxation. He has worked for large public accounting firms and international private, corporate industries. Ron is extremely knowledgeable in the areas of estate planning, investing, and strategies for maximizing your future sustainable income. He is constantly up-to-date on national and world events providing great resources for future planning. Ron's continued work and research into the ever-changing tax laws and business have made him an excellent resource for this book.

I asked Ron what the best plan for retirement is right now and his response was simple, "Live below your means. Have an emergency fund, *always*." He said that this advice works regardless of your age and that everyone should try to work down their debt.

"Those are priority," Ron said. "After your basic emergency savings, work down all of your debt, except for your mortgage unless it's possible. Work down credit card debt and student loan debt as quickly as possible."

Ron recommended that before your save for retirement, you work away your debt as quickly as possible while living below your means. After eliminating your debt, it's time to begin saving.

"The rule is six months of living expenses," recommended Ron. "If you are sharing expenses, for instance, when you are married, you can trim that down some maybe to four months since it is unlikely both of you will be out of work at the same time. Sustainable living will help determine that amount also."

When it comes to investments, Ron said there are three categories to look at: Stocks, bonds, and cash.

"Stocks can be all over the place, high risk, moderate, and low risk," said Ron. "Bonds are less risky than stocks. Cash is defined as liquid assets that can be obtained immediately such as a checking, savings account or money market account."

According to Ron, how you invest will be best gauged by what the market has been doing, what it is doing now, and how expensive it is.

"If the market has been down for three to four years, you may want to invest 70-80 percent of your total investments, if you are young," he said. "If the market has been riding high for seven or eight years, you may want to wait and invest in a less risky option, especially as you become closer to retirement. The two factors to consider here are the market trends and your age."

Ron said that the stock market is generally the best place to make investments though you need to do your research before making a decision. This is also where a financial advisor can assist you.

"You need to research and gain knowledge to wholly look at the trends," said Ron. "If the market has been gaining for seven or eight years, approximately 50-60 percent of your total investment should reflect stocks. And, the older you are, the less risk you want to take in stocks."

Individual stock investing takes an enormous amount of time and research, warned Ron. If you are interested in stock investing, he suggested immersing yourself in current trends in world news and economics. He said you should know the company and study its financial statements. It is not suggested for someone who wants to forgo the effort. Individual stock picking is a career of its own.

Ron said a few index funds and some specialty funds are typically a good option for diversifying your investments. If you wanted to concentrate in certain areas such as healthcare, technology, utilities, or commodities, there are specific funds available for each of these.

"Funds spread the risk among many companies instead of individual stock picking," said Ron. "It's an art, not a science."

Other types of investments such as starting a business or real estate can also be solid investment option, according to Ron, if you have the time and the knowledge base to do so but there are many variables involved.

"Real estate and business are careers of their own," said Ron, "but they can be profitable if you are qualified to put in the time required to manage maintenance and repairs. Outsourcing is expensive. Timing is crucial."

Ron said once you decide a good percentage balance of risk for stocks, bonds, and cash for your age and situation, you can make changes. This is known as rebalancing. For example, let's say you have determined your percentages as 65, 25, and 10 for stocks, bonds, and cash respectively. At an average of twice a year, rebalance your portfolio to these amounts as the values change. Say your stocks went up to become 75 percent of your total investment, it is time to sell 10 percent and put the profit into bonds and cash to rebalance your investments back to the original percentages. Or, if your stocks decrease by five percent for this period, you can buy good stocks at a discount by taking money from the bond funds or cash as appropriate. This is a buy and hold strategy but also allows for some trading to readjust and take profits.

As you age, the percentages of your investment portfolio will also need to change. As time goes by, you'll want to be safer with your investments and work with a higher percentage of cash.

"I take a little more risk," said Ron who is now 58. "Up until about 10 months ago, I took a lot of risk. Now I'm looking at retirement more seriously. My balance was 90 percent stocks, zero bonds, and 10 percent cash. Now it's 80 percent stocks, 10 percent bonds, and 10 percent cash. Plus, the stocks themselves have become more conservative but this is a second career passion for me."

Ron added that dividend paying stocks are worthwhile because you don't need to sell them at market price to get your profits. Since you get paid a regular profit through dividends paid by the company, you have more control as to whether to reinvest or buy elsewhere. If a company reinvests profits in itself and does not pay a regular dividend, you automatically share the company with less people regardless of profit or loss. If the stock *increases* in value, you are sharing it with less people. Conversely, if the stock *decreases* in value, you are sharing it with less people.

If your own a company does not pay a dividend, you will need to sell stock to obtain a passive income. Ron said even if the stock is a good overall investment, you will be forced to sell it. Generally, you have limited choice in your own investment without a dividend payment.

To determine if your company pays out dividends or charges you to have them, you will need to research the stock on a financial site such as Yahoo Finance. If you have a brokerage account, you will have a financial report, according to Ron. Another quick way to find this information is to visit the website for the company or mutual funds. This will also tell you about their average annual income. You will need to go to your employer's benefits website to find the management cost/fees to own this fund.

Once you retire and are ready to access your money, you will want to use it in ways to make it last. You will need to consider your personal circumstances but Ron warns against early withdraw of retirement funds.

"It is important to keep your rebalancing intact," said Ron. "Any retirement account also has an age limit to withdraw at 59 ½ years of age. If you withdraw from your retirement earlier, there are penalties and taxes to pay."

Ron advised that in order to obtain maximum tax advantages, you should be diversified with a Roth IRA, a traditional IRA, and a taxable brokerage account. This way, you can take money from three different sources and they each have different tax advantages.

"Always check with a financial advisor or a CPA for tax/retirement planning," advised Ron. "Every situation is unique and these are some general guidelines that should be followed. Laws continually change. Live below your means. I can't emphasize that enough. Make your money work for you."

Financial planning and future sustainability are personalized, thoughtful processes. After combining the previous information and the personal interview, I hope that you feel more confident in handling your money. Expect a lifelong learning curve and fluctuations in your financial education. The most efficient and safe way to financially sustain yourself is to consult with a certified financial advisor. Along with his/her advice and the tools from this chapter, you will be ready to "enjoy a lifetime in your own home."

Health Insurance

Based on many years of nursing experience, I predict that *health insurance will be the great equalizer of our collective financial futures.* It is imperative to study your health insurance to avoid the pitfall of medical costs draining down your assets. Bills quickly add up even though you have health insurance. With any insurance exceptions always outweigh the benefits offered. Insurance companies expend unlimited time, personnel, and research to tip the scales in their favor.

One of the major pitfalls of financial planning is a lack of knowledge of your insurance coverage which can lead to an increased need to draw down savings. Earlier, in "A typical hospital experience," Angelo realized that he would need a large amount of liquid assets to purchase the equipment that Marie needed to return home. Since her stroke was such a large and significant emergency, he needed to draw upon his liquid capital as fast as possible. Angelo and Marie had health insurance, yet they knew little of its intricacies. Because of this lack of knowledge, Angelo purchased items which would have been covered by his insurance. He also hired help in his home and tapped into money from his emergency fund. Comparable to most Medicare recipients, Angelo and Marie procrastinated navigating its confusing website at Medicare.gov.

Medicare

Medicare is one of the primary health insurances for people as they age. According to the site Medicare.gov, the first time you enroll in Medicare is during the initial enrollment period. There are two basic types of Medicare plans: Medicare A and B. There is also a third option called the Medicare Advantage Plan. With any of these plans there is also an additional cost for the drug plan (Medicare Part D).

According to the Medicare.gov site Medicare A and B cover approximately 80 percent of your medical costs. So with the original Medicare A and B plans there is also a supplemental option called Medigap. Medigap is an additional cost but it will pick up the 20 percent not covered by your original Medicare A or B plan. Original Medicare A and B are generally costlier options but offer you a vast number of providers across the country.

A less expensive option is the Medicare Advantage Plan which works with local HMOs and PPOs. It includes the same coverage as original Medicare, but may limit the providers to the insurance company managing the plan. For example, if Humana manages your Medicare advantage plan, you will be limited to the providers offered by the Humana insurance company in your area. If you have an emergency outside of your coverage area, this will be considered an out of network expense. Also, Medigap is not available to someone with a Medicare Advantage Plan.

"For example, if you're eligible for Medicare when you turn 65, you can sign up during the 7-month period that:
- Begins 3 months before the month you turn 65
- Includes the month you turn 65
- Ends 3 months after the month you turn 65," according to Medicare.gov (Part A & Part B sign up periods, 2019).

It is imperative that you enroll during this period to avoid a penalty.

"You usually don't pay a monthly premium for Medicare Part A (Hospital Insurance) coverage if you or your spouse paid Medicare taxes for a certain amount of time while working. This is sometimes called 'premium-free Part A'" according to Medicare.gov (Part A & Part B sign up periods, 2019).

"You can get premium-free Part A at 65 if:
- You already get retirement benefits from Social Security or the Railroad Retirement Board.
- You're eligible to get Social Security or Railroad benefits but haven't filed for them yet.
- You or your spouse had Medicare-covered government employment" according to Medicare.gov (Part A costs, 2019).

"If you're under 65, you can get premium-free Part A if:
- You got Social Security or Railroad Retirement Board disability benefits for 24 months.
- You have End-Stage Renal Disease (ESRD) and meet certain requirements," according to Medicare.gov (Part A costs, 2019).
-

Part A Premiums

"If you buy Part A, you'll pay up to $437 each month. If you paid Medicare taxes for less than 30 quarters, the standard Part A premium is $437. If you paid Medicare taxes for 30-39 quarters, the standard Part A premium is $240" (Part A costs, 2019).

"In most cases, if you choose to buy Part A, you must also:
- Have Medicare Part B (Medical Insurance)
- Pay monthly premiums for both Part A and Part B" according Medicare.gov (Part A costs, 2019).

-

"In general, Part A covers:

- Inpatient care in a hospital
- Skilled nursing facility care
- Inpatient care in a skilled nursing facility (not custodial or long-term care)
- Hospice care
- Home health care" according to Medicare.gov (What Part A Covers, 2019).

"Part B covers 2 types of services

- **Medically necessary services:** Services or supplies that are needed to diagnose or treat your medical condition and that meet accepted standards of medical practice.
- **Preventive services:** Health care to prevent illness (like the flu) or detect it at an early stage, when treatment is most likely to work best," according to Medicare.gov (What Part B Covers, 2019).
-

"You pay nothing for most preventive services if you get the services from a health care provider who accepts assignment," (What Part B Covers, 2019).

"Part B covers things like:

- Clinical research
- Ambulance services
- Durable medical equipment (DME)
- Mental health
    - Inpatient
    - Outpatient
    - Partial hospitalization
- Getting a second opinion before surgery

- Limited outpatient prescription drugs" according to Medicare.gov (What Part B Covers, 2019).

Know Your Coverage

I started researching this for my own benefit and for the benefit of my patients. I went to the Medicare.gov website and entered my zip code to get started. I found that many of my patients were not aware of the type of Medicare they had or what it covered. Learning about your medical insurance is not a process you want to begin during a hospitalization. You should know your coverage *before* a medical crisis occurs. Through my research I found many patients were surprised by the benefits they were actually getting compared to the costs that they were paying for a Medicare plan.

In my research, I found that Medicare payments depend on the area in which you live and your current health status. So, for example, in my situation I found that straight Medicare with the drug plan in my area for a person in good health would cost $5,486.40 per person per year, according to Medicare.gov.

The Medicare Advantage Plan was another alternative. It was limited by the insurance company with which you choose to allocate your Medicare benefits. A general Medicare advantage plan with a drug plan for a person in good health cost $4,236.00 per person per year, according to Medicare.gov.

Get What You Need

Assess your health situation currently and the risks and benefits of your health insurance plan as it is now. The alternatives and health insurances available are numerous and should be tailored to your personal situation.

Learn the Terms of the Industry

In order to choose the best health insurance option, familiarize yourself with terms such as deductible, coinsurance, co-pays, and lifetime maximum benefit. Remember these actions are a process so there's no need to hastily rush through selecting a plan. The insurance companies create their policies with years of forethought and complication. Start with basic definitions of their terms and soon the language will become clearer.

Basic Term to Know

Here is a brief synopsis of common insurance terms according to Blue Cross Blue Shield of Michigan insurance at the company website at www.bcbsm.com/index/health-insurance.

Deductible

"A deductible is the amount you pay for health care services before your health insurance begins to pay.

How it works: If your plan's deductible is $1,500, you'll pay 100 percent of eligible health care expenses until the bills total $1,500. After that, you share the cost with your plan by paying coinsurance," (How do deductibles, coinsurance and copays work, 2019).

Coinsurance

"Coinsurance is your share of the costs of a health care service. It's usually figured as a percentage of the amount we allow to be charged for services. You start paying coinsurance after you've paid your plan's deductible.

How it works: You've paid $1,500 in health care expenses and met your deductible. When you go to the doctor, instead of paying all costs, you and your plan share the cost. For example, your plan pays 70 percent. The 30 percent you pay is your coinsurance"

(How do deductibles, coinsurance and copays work, 2019).

Copay

"A copay is a fixed amount you pay for a health care service, usually when you receive the service. The amount can vary by the type of service.

How it works: Your plan determines what your copay is for different types of services, and when you have one. You may have a copay before you've finished paying toward your deductible. You may also have a copay after you pay your deductible, and when you owe coinsurance" (How do deductibles, coinsurance and copays work, 2019).

Scrutinize your health insurance policy for hidden costs. Learn the acronyms. Learn the risks. This is a great task which I find to be worth the time to investigate your health insurance plan and its alignment with your current needs.

Based on your current health, do your best to anticipate your future needs. For example, a healthier person may want a high deductible plan with a health savings account option. A less healthy person may want a safer plan with a higher per month cost. There are many options which can be balanced considering your budget and health condition.

Angelo found that he needed to quickly learn about his health insurance. As in most parts of this book, you will find that enjoying a lifetime in your own home is specific to your own personalized needs. Continue to investigate your health insurance needs and weigh their costs and benefits. Once you select a health insurance plan, be sure to watch for changes to your plan as they can change often.

A healthy financial plan should encompass all aspects of your life: savings, budgeting, investing, and the all-important cost of health insurance. As with any other journey in life, tread lightly. Consider the time you have dedicated to earning money and planning your future. In the areas of stability and economic growth, reflect upon your past views of money. In order to enjoy a lifetime in your own home, financial matters rank high on the scale of significance. So, in order to properly manage your wealth, stroll with purpose through this chapter and the rest of the book one step at a time.

As I said earlier in this chapter, *health insurance will be the great equalizer of our collective financial futures*.

5

HOMECARE FOR BASIC NECESSITIES

This chapter takes real-life scenarios to help you understand how to obtain homecare resources. These resources include nursing services, custodial services, specialty physicians, and specialty testing sites. This chapter will also discuss the importance of expanding your knowledge and having a willingness to learn.

The Cowboy

Today, Arizona still reeks of thick-skinned cowboys and the Old West. As a result, I had the pleasure of meeting one of the oldest and toughest rodeo cowboys that I had ever seen. His full-time occupation was riding and roping large, dangerous cattle. His face and skin were as weathered as the cracked, dry Arizona desert.

Standing at only about 5-foot 6 inches, he swaggered, creating a huge presence in our unit. His confident stature gave me pause and I instantly understood how his presence allowed him to handle these dangerous animals. He was a true cowboy. His name was Al.

Al was in the hospital for the first time in his adult life. He was admitted to the EENT (Ear, Eyes, Nose, and Throat) surgical unit preoperatively. He was having great difficulty with swallowing and tumors in his throat were the cause. His surgery was scheduled in the morning so he was preadmitted due to bleeding in his throat.

Al returned to our unit after his subsequent surgery and time in the post anesthesia unit. At first, I barely recognized him. He had the usual litany of tubes and drains, including a nasogastric feeding tube, and a tracheostomy (a breathing cannula originating from the trachea via a stoma through the neck).

As with most of our patients, he needed round-the-clock monitoring. Frequent suctioning was needed to keep his tracheostomy patent (open). Drainage bulbs coming from his neck were continuously filling with blood. The nasogastric feeding tube required continuous monitoring as well. When he arrived back at our unit, Al was also hooked up to telemetry (continuous cardiac monitoring).

I don't think this cowboy had ever expected himself to be in this vulnerable state. Al was a very ornery patient due to this fact. He consistently pulled on his tubes and lines and he was angry with his situation. No one could have prepared him for his postsurgical state. He had lived a life of complete control and independence. His postsurgical experience robbed him of the life he knew.

As his condition improved and many of the lines and drains had been discontinued, he anticipated going home. Al still had a tracheostomy and the feeding tube in place, however. As his case manager at the time, I was given the usual list of equipment supplies and care that he would need. It was one of the longest lists I had ever seen.

The items on the list included an emergency trach, a portable suction machine, a sterile trach cleaning kit, humidified oxygen with a condenser, trach ties, and sterile water. The tube feeding supplies included a specialized feeding formula, tubing, feeding pump, and a tube feeding kit for flushing the system. His condition was so weak that he also needed a wheelchair and a walker.

On his list of services were homecare nursing, physical therapy, and a home health aide. These services were usually all provided by a local home care agency and all of the durable medical equipment listed above would usually be provided by a medical supply company.

Surprisingly, many of our patients with similar surgeries have been able to return home. With assistance, many patients can manage, especially if they are decannulated (removal of the tracheostomy) before discharge. Decannulation was not attainable for this cowboy. If his circumstances were different, he would have been able to return home, but, unfortunately, this was not the case.

This man lived in a very remote area on a ranch. His address was stated as "Highway 89." He described to me that access to his property required going to the local saloon and getting the key to the gate at the entrance to his ranch. He did not have a house number or a street address.

As his case manager, I searched for companies covered by his insurance that were willing to visit his home. There was a durable medical equipment (DME) company in his area but they were unwilling to go to a saloon for access to his property. Medical products companies need to deliver to the patient directly to ensure no mishaps occurs. The home care agencies did not cover such a large, remote geographic area. Options for this rugged, independent man were becoming limited.

I brought him lists of long-term acute care facilities. Al vehemently bargained with me to return to his home. I assured him that I had searched every avenue for him to be able to return home but, due to his very remote location and lack of access to services, Al would need to choose a long-term acute care facility.

I knew that if he was not able to tolerate decannulation before his discharge, he had a great chance of keeping the tracheostomy long-term. Once admitted to a long-term acute care facility, the chances of his breathing on his own again deteriorated. Long-term acute care facilities care for gravely disabled patients in a sub acute hospital-type setting. Secretly, I contemplated the sad fate of this cowboy, physically and emotionally.

The doctors attempted to remove the tracheostomy several times without success. In this patient's case, even without the tracheostomy he could not have returned home. Al's severely remote living situation and difficult access to his location made it very unlikely that he would ever return to his former life.

Lessons Learned- Location, Location, Location

The first three rules for real estate are location, location, location. As I saw this poor man's life change forever, I reflected on my own situation. Did I live in an area that was accessible to medical care? Do you? Do you live in an urban, suburban, or rural setting? Each of these has their advantages and disadvantages.

Living in Rural Settings

A rural setting enables more freedom in redecorating and remodeling your home according to your needs. Most rural areas do not have the homeowner's association rules and the strict zoning regulations which you must abide by. Without these rules, it is easier to remodel your home for an enriched lifelong future without stipulation. You can add ramps and outbuildings and any other structures you may need as you age without significant intrusion from regulation. And, since you are further away from many services, chances are you have a strong group of self-reliant neighbors at your disposal. Rural living fosters independence and interdependence. However, the drawback is being a great distance from services such as hospitals and specialists.

As you saw in the previous story, this very strong and

independent rodeo cowboy faced a drastically altered life due to several reasons, one of which being the location of his residence. If you live in a sparsely populated area, consider alternative plans for healthcare. Perhaps plan meet-up groups with your neighbors to discuss this issue. The combined effort of your neighbors with similar concerns will lead to alternatives in healthcare in your area. For example, simply creating better signage and improving access roads to the community would preempt a health crisis for everyone. In addition, map the area surrounding your town and become knowledgeable about the closest resources and the services they provide.

Living in Suburban & Urban Settings

In a suburban or an urban setting, your chances to accessing healthcare improve greatly. Thirty to 45 minutes is a good general time frame in which to get to a hospital. Less than 30 minutes is most advantageous.

Map out a 30-minute radius from your home and locate all the hospitals, doctor's offices, specialists, labs, and agencies available. Consider the types of services surrounding you. What do each of these medical facilities provide? This may seem like an extraordinary task and possibly an unnecessary one but, as you have seen in the previous story, access to health care turns out to be priority one when you are facing the possibility of having to leave your home for an institution.

Having a knowledge of your surrounding resources gives you an advantage to aging in place. Do you have a primary care physician? Primary care physicians are required to obtain home health services. Are they located close by? Also locate other facilities including dialysis centers, home care agencies, physical, occupational, and speech therapy locations. Become aware of vision care, dental care, and other preventative care facilities within your general area. All of this information will provide insight as to whether you are in the proper location for enjoying a lifetime in your own home.

Amenities

As a case manager, I met hundreds of people from all over the country. In Arizona and other states, the in-depth assessment required of the patient's home setting was surprising. Due to the increase in the number of resources required for home care, my assessment also needed to include the basic needs of home living. I found myself asking about reliable sources of water and energy. Especially in remote areas of the country, some homes are not prewired for basic survival. Clean, running water, refrigeration, and sewers suddenly became interest for me when discharging someone to home care.

Many of the services provided by home health require an adequate abundance of resources in a person's home. For example, home infusion is getting very popular. Hospitals realize that they can discharge people early to their homes for their remaining course of intravenous antibiotics. Courses of antibiotics can run for six to eight weeks or longer. Other sustaining medications can be delivered intravenously at home for an unlimited amount of time. For example dopamine, dobutamine, and milrinone are given for heart failure. Administering IV medications at home requires a clean environment, proper refrigeration, clean water, and the appropriate care of supplies.

Do you have a reliable source of water, sewer, and power? Are any of these services to your home in need of repair? Do you have the knowledge to maintain these services? Do you know where to power on and off services such as natural gas? Has the weather affected any of your basic needs while you have been in hospital? These are the questions that I often face as an RN delivering services to patient's homes.

Many agencies have become very concerned with safety for their nurses. This is another issue which you should consider when planning a potential need for home care. Is your home in a safe location? Would an agency be tentative about sending a nurse or therapist to your home? Do you have appropriate lighting and access to your front entrance? If your home or neighborhood is deemed unsafe for home care, will an agency reconsider sending any professional to your home? This single factor may completely destroy your chances of getting home care, especially if your insurance covers a limited amount of home care agencies.

Home Care Benefits

In Chapter 4, I touched upon health insurance. I would suggest an in-depth study of your home care benefits through your health insurance company. Most plans including Medicare provide a home health benefit. However, this benefit may be limited due to your circumstances, specific requirements, and medications.

As with most insurance companies, your coverage will not be specifically explained to you unless you ask questions. There are many exceptions and clauses which you may need to verify in order to get the best care. Again, I cannot stress how important it is to have a thorough understanding of your health insurance.

Transportation Benefits

Each step in the discharge process requires some preplanning. When you are urgently sent to the hospital, the last thing on your mind is your transportation home. You can save a great deal of money and stress with awareness of your insurance transportation benefits.

Remember, the transportation required could be more complicated than a simple taxi ride. For example, a patient with a tracheostomy would require humidification, suction, and possibly oxygen to transfer locations. Surgical and orthopedic patients may require a handicap vehicle or a large occupancy vehicle for their transfer. A medical transport may be necessary.

Does your insurance cover these kind of transports? A simple discharge ride home could cost thousands of dollars without a pre-investigation of your specific insurance coverage.

In addition to the stress of hospitalization hundreds of miles from home, one of my patients requested discharge as soon as possible. He and his wife were on vacation and had insurance from their home state of residence which did not transfer to our state. The man demanded immediate transfer home due to his lack of insurance in Arizona.

The couple knew that every day of his hospitalization was mounting bills which they could not afford but in order to transfer this orthopedic patient back to his state of residence, he would need to be immobilized. His wife also needed transportation. Due to his fragile state and emergent surgery, we were unable to arrange transport through his insurance because of the possibility of extreme medical complications such as paralysis. His accident had left this couple without insurance coverage and under extreme stress in a foreign state. This is just one example of the importance of studying your health insurance and all of its intricacies.

Willingness, Determination, and Skill Development

During your hospital experience, you will be exposed to unknown procedures, tests, and an entirely new vocabulary. Your background information regarding your insurance and your further determination to acquire skills and knowledge will help you greatly. This is a time of stress, anxiety, and fear.

One of the suggestions I give my patients is to be your own best advocate. In Chapter 2, you may have realized that great support is needed in this area due to your strained condition. Therefore, if you are unable to be your own best advocate at this time, you will need outside support to be your advocate during your hospital stay.

As a bedside nurse and as a case manager, it gives me increased comfort and hope for a patient's recovery when I can explain their procedures and discharge instructions to an involved family member or friend. Your advocate can interpret your home care needs with clarity and subjectivity. In most cases they will be the people following you home and involving themselves in your continued care. They can learn from the professionals at the hospital including the physical and occupational therapists, nurses, and doctors. Ask many questions, pay attention, and practice manual feedback demonstration of your abilities to be sure to learn about your care adequately.

Home care requires willingness, determination, and knowledge. The therapy professionals and nurses will visit you in your home likely two to three times a week for 30 to 90 minutes. This leaves the remaining responsibility to you and your caregiver. Therefore, while you are in hospital, you and your advocate should practice your caregiving skills. This is especially important if you're leaving the hospital with home infusion, needs for wound care, and equipment. I have seen incredibly devoted family members who were determined to confidently learn sophisticated procedures in order to take their loved one home.

Since hospitals are under great pressure to discharge in a timely manner, home infusion, wound care, and equipment have been streamlined in their design for easier, more-friendly use. Nurses and therapists have been well-versed in teaching patients and families for home care. Outside homecare agencies and infusion companies are also experts in this area. Your caregiver should feel comfortable performing these skills in managing your equipment before you leave the hospital. This will make the transition exponentially easier for you and your family.

By this time, the hospital discharge procedure may sound very overwhelming especially in complicated situations. Luckily, home care agencies and infusion companies have developed extremely user-friendly procedures and equipment. As a homecare nurse, I have been amazed at the ease of transition for most of the families independent of their previous experience. I have encountered many caregiver family members with no previous medical experience that fare extremely well. Your home environment is the safest environment to avoid complications such as infections. It is possible to comfortably recover at home without complications with diligent caregivers and family members to help.

Services Available at Home

Based on your diagnosis and/or complications, your insurance will only cover your designated length of stay in the hospital for so long. These cost containment measures encourage hospitals to discharge patients in a timely manner but then much responsibility falls upon the caregivers whose vested interest drives them to do a fabulous job.

The list of services available for home care are endless and grows continuously, making it easier for hospitals to discharge patients. Many home care services are covered by insurance and may have a co-pay. The payments to the hospital or agencies for home care services rely on a patient's diagnosis.

Wound Care

Wound care is among the most popular homecare service provide today. Wound care can be as simple as a dry sterile dressing or as complicated as negative pressure wound vacuum assisted closure (VAC) therapy. In either of these situations, a setup area and supplies will be necessary, along with some training. The home care agency costs usually include providing wound care supplies unless there are specialty items excluded from your policy.

I have seen cases of wound care on all levels from acute abdominal wounds to vascular cases with compression wraps. In the area of wound care, maintaining proper healing of affected areas involves a learning process of watch, do, and teach. You will be required to watch the nursing staff preform the proper wound care technique, do it yourself, and teach it back to the nurses before discharge.

Supplies

You will also be taught to handle supplies with a clean technique and securement devices. Postsurgical wound care could possibly also include drainage devices, sutures, staples, and more complicated chest-tube-like apparatuses. The home health agency will provide the tools and training necessary for this. You will have access to the nurses and urgent situations when a wound is compromised. This access is usually 24/7 by phone and nursing visits will be provided as necessary.

Postsurgical care may also include orthopedic therapies, airway maintenance devices, and durable medical equipment. Physical therapy, occupational therapy, and speech therapy are all available as homecare services. Airway maintenance as far as tracheostomy care is usually provided by nurses and taught to families.

The durable medical equipment involved post-surgically could range from tracheostomy supplies, ambulatory and non-ambulatory assistive devices, canes, walkers, and wheelchairs. Oxygen, various tubing, and pumps for IV infusion or enteral feedings may also be taught. For this reason, I again stress the importance of learning the intricacies of your personal health insurance policy. Most supplies are covered by insurances unless they are supplementary for comfort.

Home Infusion Services

Another common homecare service that's growing in use daily are home infusion services. Home infusion is usually administering medication, nutrition, or other fluids through a type of central line. Infusion services are extremely user-friendly and can be easily adaptable for home use.

The delivery systems for your medication range from self-regulating "elastomeric" medicine balls to simple infusion pumps.

Due to the length of treatment, the most common medications administered at home are antibiotics. Fluids, chemotherapy, adrenergics, total parenteral nutrition (total nutrition through an IV line), and many others fall into this category.

Acquiring the skills to administer intravenous drugs in a clean, appropriate environment will allow you to recover in your own home rather than spending a possible six to eight weeks in a nursing home. It also reduces your chances of experiencing a secondary infection.

Chronic Conditions

Due to the nature of chronic conditions such as chronic obstructive pulmonary disease (COPD), diabetes, heart failure, kidney failure, and liver failure, home care is essential. Managing chronic illnesses most likely will include long-term homecare. For example, patients with kidney failure are maintaining their dialysis at home. COPD patients likely have home oxygen, humidity, and/or a continuous positive pressure airway system. Chronic systolic heart failure patients are leaving the hospital with left ventricular assist devices (partial artificial heart devices) or total artificial heart devices.

Hospice

Hospice is another irreplaceable homecare service. Patients can receive pain management and end-of-life services per their wishes with the comfort of their family surrounding them. Hospice services have expanded into the home setting offering various spiritual, mental, and social support with clergy, nurses, and various therapies to aid the dying process.

All of these diagnoses and many more can be treated safely at home. However, the transition from hospital to home can be complicated. Proactively planning for these eventualities provides an easy and comfortable recovery. It also avoids any chance of needing institutionalized care.

Other Services to Consider

Think about the day-to-day upkeep in your home as it is now. To ensure a smooth transition from the hospital to home, set up other services to make your daily responsibilities easier so you can concentrate on your recovery. These services may range from someone preparing your meals to doing your laundry and maintenance of lawn care to housekeeping. In preparation for a long-term future in your home be aware of the services in your area. Neighbors and friends can help give referrals because they have probably had similar situations occur.

Some specific home health agencies offer custodial care. Custodial care refers to activities of daily living and other non-nursing needs. These needs would be defined as companion care, bathing, cooking, cleaning, laundry, transportation, and respite care for family members. Most of these homecare agencies are privately paid for by the patients as these services are deemed not medically necessary by insurance companies. Health insurance will only pay for services they deem medically necessary.

Frequent hospitalizations, which often happen concurrently, will derail your regular schedule. Consider other services to streamline your daily responsibilities such as setting up regularly scheduled maintenance. For example, using the free bill pay services at most major banks will send you reminders when your bills are due. As you saw in "A Typical Hospital Experience," when a crisis occurs your sense of time will be interrupted and you may not remember your day-to-day routines. Therefore, it would be much easier to have these services to remind and care for you.

Regional Considerations

Depending on the area of the country you live in, there will be specific services you may need. During the winter months, it may be necessary to employ snow removal services and de-icing of your home to improve access. As I mentioned previously, access to your home is paramount to receiving services in a timely manner or even at all. Even in a non-crisis situation, heavy tasks such as shoveling snow and winterizing your home can be physically challenging as you get older.

Take Arizona as an example. Due to the large number of retirees in Arizona, an abundance of these services exist. Much of our lawn care is minimized with xeriscaping and irrigation. Most major pharmacies in Arizona and across the country offer regular services with automatic refills of medication and pre-packaging with dates and times if needed.

Regardless of what area you live in, most large grocery chains offer delivery services or preorders online with pickup at the store. Consider alternative transportation services such as Uber and Lyft to minimize the amount of trips away from home during your recovery. Awareness of these other services and preplanning will ease your mind during this chaotic time.

Preplanning Homecare

Preplanning for proper homecare will minimize your chances of being sent to a nursing home. Each of the services you will require can be set up in advance to ease the transition home. This is especially true if you experience frequent reoccurring admissions to the hospital over a short timeframe.

Due to the financial penalties for early readmission, hospitals are enforcing safe discharges strategically to reduce concurrent stays. For you and your family, this translates into a possibility of institutional placement if you are not prepared for homecare. At the time of your discharge, ask questions and grasp a good understanding of your continued care and medications. Case managers are pressured to send patients home to an environment which is not dangerous, ensures proper care, and a low probability of readmission. Their faith in your plan for homecare will determine your future destination.

The Ten Commandments of Home Care

1. Know thy health insurance.
2. Bring an advocate.
3. Have a plan and a ride home.

4. Negotiate your discharge plan (such as scheduling follow-up appointments).

5. Take stock of your assets (your existing home environment).

6. Learn your aftercare including procedures.

7. Research and memorize your medications.

8. Have your paperwork in order including a living will and a medical power of attorney.

9. Contain liquid capital expenditures.

10. Prepare for change with a positive attitude.

6

FUTUROLOGY

A Vision of a Typical *Future* Home Experience: Livia's Story

"I just arrived home last night after a mobile cardiac catheterization following my heart attack," said Livia. "I got the stents placed in my heart just in time thanks to 24-hour home EKG monitoring. It all happened so fast. Now I'm feeling so much relief from the chest pain. All I'm left with is a pinpoint incision in my wrist. My EKG and vital signs will continue to be monitored as well as my incision site from my home for as long as necessary. I know that I will have to take it easy for the next few days."

When Livia awoke the morning after her medical emergency, she felt it might have been a dream. Things were just as normal as they always were with the help of her smart home.

"Thanks to my smart home, my morning routine was preset," Livia said. "The opacity and brightness of the lighting, the temperature, the alarms, and the security settings were maintained. My personal digital assistant reminded me of today's activities. I was due to tutor a student via hologram, so I needed to get ready for the day."

Livia said her smart bed voiced a concern that her sleep pattern was unusual. She admitted that she did feel somewhat weak to start off her daily routine, so she decided to use her conveyance to move her through the washing and drying stages as preset in the shower.

"Today, I was especially thankful for the safety of a heated dry floor and intense lighting to assist with my grooming," said Livia. "According to my smart mirror and scale, all of my health indicators were normal."

As she made her way into the kitchen, Livia's digital assistant informed her of the changes in her menu and medications for the day. She was dispensed one new medication with its litany of information. She has also been prescribed a cardiac diet. At her request, the smart refrigerator eliminated all the restricted foods from its inventory list. She advised her personal digital assistant to create the most flavorful breakfast available within the restrictions of her new diet.

After breakfast, Livia's assistant informed her of a new activity on her agenda. She has been prescribed a 30-minute physical regimen with continuous health monitoring and graded effort.

"I headed towards my three-dimensional smart theater to choose my activity," said Livia. "I decided to ski the Swiss Alps. When I placed my finger on the handles of the exercise machine, my labs were monitored. From my identifying fingerprint, I was organized with a familiar support group. We had an invigorating experience, and, at the finish, we celebrated by comparing our results."

In today's world, at the age of 120, a major heart event posed insignificant changes to Livia's routine.

"Later today, after my work, I will be taking the hyper loop to visit my great-great-grandchildren in Texas (a 500-mile trip)," added Livia. "But this time, just as a precaution, I will wear my health monitoring devices on the way. I can't wait to tell them about my trip to Switzerland."

The Future of Technology

What you have just read is the experience of someone aging in place in the future. Contemplate what the world will be like in 20 years. A great deal of changes are being made every day in future technology to assist us at home.

Even in the last 20 years, futuristic products which make our life easier have multiplied exponentially. I've done a great deal of research to explore the possibilities of staying a lifetime in your home with the use of future inventions. As you know, computers and the internet offer unlimited knowledge on any subject and the ability to easily research.

Learning to Use Computers & the Internet

Depending on your experience with computer programs and the internet, you can access the necessities to easily take you through your natural life at home. If you are unfamiliar with the use of technology, there are many ways you can expand your knowledge.

Limitless classes are offered. People without computer experience at every level can become familiar with the trends of the future. You can find these classes at local libraries, community colleges, and even senior-living facilities.

Recall the information in Chapter 5 regarding home care basic necessities. A willingness, determination, and skill development are mandatory for aging in place. Computer and internet use will be an inescapable necessity to upkeep your future in your own home.

Through my many interviews with the greatest generation, I learned of an interesting trend. I was surprised by my discussions when I found that this generation had great faith in their doctors. At the time of their youth, it was common for the family doctor to visit them in their home. As a result of this trust, the family doctor was a professional and a friend.

Many of my interviewees expected their doctors to teach them about new technology in the world, specifically the internet. This sounded unrealistic to me, but to this generation, a doctor represented a trusted resource of this valued information. Undoubtedly, he or she he would teach them. Today, it would be highly unlikely that any doctor would provide this service.

It is not necessary to be a professional information technologist or software programmer to learn the basics of technology. Use of computers, the internet, and applications is continuously becoming more effortless and user friendly.

Technology is also taking into account the ways in which people learn. If you are a visual or auditory learner, computer programs, applications, and screen formats have been designed to adapt to your capabilities. If you are a person who needs to continually practice learning new technology, it is wise to take a series of classes and be involved with groups who regularly practice. This is also an excellent way to expand your social circle.

In addition to using your desktop or laptop as avenues for learning technology, phones, tablets, and even television screens can be used. For instance, smart phones and smart televisions have become an accessible lifeline to information. With one or two clicks, we are moments away from any service or entertainment needed to enrich our lives. The internet provides immediate information, fulfilling our urgent needs. Thus, the information superhighway will greatly enhance aging in place.

If any of these devices aren't familiar to you, I highly recommend that you take advantage of this technology and put aside your fears. Embrace the wave the future has to offer.

Of course, this is not limited to computer technology. It also applies to medical technology, transportation devices, entertainment, and many other services which you can take advantage of. Hopefully, many of these devices and services will already be familiar to you.

The Future of Transportation

Through my interviews, I discovered the highest priorities for older people who were remaining in their own homes. I anticipated an answer in the realm of acquiring food for personal care. Surprisingly, the first thing on their list was transportation to the doctor's office. Transportation presented a significant problem especially for those unable to drive at some point.

As you age, you may need to travel more frequently to several different doctors due to the expansion of specialty medicine. Specialized outpatient therapies may also require numerous visits for maximum rehabilitation. Newer, less expensive options exist for transportation which are overtaking taxis and private chauffeurs. Lyft and Uber have made single passenger transportation to an exact location an affordable possibility. Their rates are cheaper than most other private transportation services.

Targeted transportation is also available through van and shuttle services. These are usually used for smaller groups for rideshare to airport or events. I predict all of these options will become more specific and eco-friendlier. The future of transportation is headed towards mass transit integrated with direct personalization. Research shows that transportation options are headed in every direction.

My vision of future infrastructure features freeways and byways exclusively for the public and autonomous vehicles. The transportation needs of the baby boomer and millennial populations will meld together. This will mean reaching "peak car" earlier than expected.

According to *The Audiopedia*, "peak car" is the theory that motor vehicle distance travel per capita, predominantly by private car, has peaked to a sustainable level (2017). Traffic fell during the "Great Recession" of 2008 and reductions were seen in Australia, Japan, and the United States. While a 2013 study showed distance travel in the U.S. declined, traffic is expected to increase as the economy improves (The Audiopedia, 2017).

"Peak car" may mean increased traffic congestion. This means that in the future it may be more difficult to get to your destination by car with an increase in road traffic. I'm sure this has happened to you at some point already.

While a new mindset is fast approaching, the great leap through the generation gap will be complicated. The independence of operating your personal automobile will battle high-tech resolutions. Ultimately, I believe "peak car" will force the hand of drivers. Research anticipates a growth in the human population due to an increase in longevity which easily translates into a need for new modes of transportation.

Uber, the Hyperloop, and Autonomous Cars: Oh, My!

Lyft, Uber, and other transportation services will solve some of these issues, but more sophisticated inventions are on the horizon. The Hyperloop is a new mode of transportation first envisioned by Tesla and SpaceX CEO Elon Musk. It consists of a low-pressure environment in the form of a tube in which pods travel at high-speed. The article states potential U.S. routes for the Hyperloop, which has a top speed of 700 mph, include major cities in several states including Colorado, Texas, Washington, Missouri, California, Florida, and Massachusetts (Lambert, 2017).

While you may not need to get to the doctor that quickly, visiting the grandchildren would be much more expedient.

Several months ago, I rented a car for an extensive vacation. I immediately noticed the changes and upgrades in this new vehicle. When I started the car, the doors locked automatically. When I did not fasten my seatbelt immediately, a blaring warning came from the dashboard. I turned on the radio and attempted to back out of the parking lot. Once I put the car in reverse, a camera appeared in front of me to show me what I was backing into and the volume on my radio was suddenly lowered. I was intrigued by some of these changes as I started driving down the street.

This minimal, semi-autonomous assistant reminded me that I was not as good a driver as I had thought. As soon as I had I entered the lane towards my destination, an annoying beeping/buzzing sound randomly appeared. I realized that every time I drifted over the lane line, this sound would remind me. As well as with the other semi-autonomous features, this vehicle prompted me to be more attentive of my own skills. At that point, I could definitely see the future of a car's decision-making capacity overriding my own.

Currently, there is a wave of continuously improving semi-autonomous vehicles being tested on roadways across America. Take Tesla for example.

"A new report now estimates that Tesla has accumulated over 1.2 billion miles on Autopilot and more than twice that when accounting for mileage in 'shadow mode'," according to an online piece from *Electrek*. "To be clear, that's the mileage driven with autopilot activated. Back in 2016, Tesla already had 1.3 billion miles driven with vehicles equipped with Autopilot. Tesla can still use data from those miles, but it's not the same has mileage driven with Autopilot on" (Lambert, 2018).

The advent of self-driving vehicles is also in the trial stages and should be widely available in the next few years. Waymo, the former Google self-driving project, has driven eight million miles on public roads using autonomous vehicles, according to another online article from *TechCrunch*. The same piece states that Waymo's fleet of self-driving vehicles is now logging 25,000 miles every day on public roads (Korosec, 2018).

The introduction of completely self-driving vehicles arriving concurrently with an aging population may be a blessing in disguise. Maintaining and enjoying a lifetime in your own home should not be a socially isolating experience. A new generation will need to part with identifying freedom through manually driven vehicles. Embracing the future of new transportation options will eliminate many barriers to maintaining a future in your current residence.

When I drove the rental car, I imagined the benefits of a completely autonomous vehicle. Freedom from traffic tickets and parking difficulties immediately came to mind. There would be continuous ridesharing, lower costs, and less stress associated with the upkeep and maintenance of juggling several vehicles. Also, there will be no need for wasted real estate devoted to parking. Traffic signals would be a thing of the past due to continuous flow and 360-degree monitoring. "Peak car" would defer to autonomous cars. These self-driving cars would never be empty or idle. This would result in halving useless pick up and drop off trips. So, when the dreaded time approaches for me to give up my car, these autonomous vehicles will be a viable alternative resulting in less stress and more freedom.

The Future of Delivery Services

You are likely familiar with phone-initiated food delivery services. For example, there's a restaurant you like so you call the company, place an order, and it's delivered directly to your home.

This has been common practice with restaurants in the pizza and Chinese food industries for some time.

Many people are now also turning to the internet to order in food from a wide variety of restaurants. Larger companies such as McDonald's, Taco Bell, and Wendy's have joined the trend and have expanded their delivery services through what have become known as aggregators.

"Aggregators build on the traditional model for food delivery, offering access to multiple restaurants through a single online portal. By logging in to the site or the app, consumers can quickly compare menus, prices, and reviews from peers. The aggregators collect a fixed margin of the order, which is paid by the restaurant, and the restaurant handles the actual delivery. There is no additional cost to the consumer" (Hirschberg, Rajko, Schumacher, & Wrulich, 2016). Some examples of such aggregators with easy-to-use apps include Uber Eats, Grubhub, and Just Eat.

Food isn't the only thing being delivered directly to consumers these days. Other delivery services on the horizon are making deliveries more personalized and faster than ever before. Thanks to online shopping apps such as Amazon, delivery of any imaginable item is currently available right to your doorstep at an increasingly rapid pace in an increasingly shorter timeframe. Forget downtime waiting for the delivery truck. Life in your own home will be enhanced by the supply all goods and services at your fingertips. The end result is less congestion on the road and faster service.

"Workhorse Group, a maker of electric delivery trucks used by UPS and FedEx, demonstrated drone deliveries launched from the roof of its vehicles at PackExpo, the biannual show dedicated to the packaging and processing industries" according to an article for the *Las Vegas Review-Journal* online (Prince, 2017).

According to another online article on *Insider Trends*, a company called Mole Solutions is developing "A freight pipeline system concept designed to move goods in customized capsules travelling under full automatic control, it's being developed to sit alongside or under existing and planned transport infrastructures" (Trotter, 2015).

From the comfort of your lift recliner, you can place an online order now and the options for ordering are only expected to expand. Simply choose any item and have a super-fast and accurate delivery.

Homes of the Future

Futurology has fast forwarded the mindset of home as well. Since your home will be the settling place for all aspects of life, frequent transportation needs may decrease substantially. As we saw earlier in this chapter, the home of the future will relieve your burdens and serve you.

"Smart Home" is the term commonly used to define a residence that has fully-automated appliances and systems that are capable of communicating with one another and can be controlled remotely by a time schedule, from any room in the home, and remotely from any location in the world by phone or internet. Such smart homes can control appliances and systems such as:

- Lighting
- Heating & Air Conditioning
- TVs
- Computers
- Entertainment
- Audio & Video Systems
- Security
- Camera Systems
- Personal Calendars & Reminders

- Irrigation System

Smart home technology offers worthwhile tools to investigate if you are truly dedicated to spending a lifetime in your own home. Based on my research, I am predicting that "smart" innovations will make your future home a personalized sanctuary. Future trends towards personalization lead me to envision a home that welcomes you and your family as a retreat from a chaotic world. And, as we all face the accommodations needed for aging in place, smart homes will become invaluable necessities as personal assistants. Smart homes offer a sensible investment when you consider their 24/7 capabilities.

Your pre-existing home can be converted into a smart home with relatively small changes. You need not upgrade all of your existing hardware and appliances to take advantage of this new technology. One area at a time can be adjusted from a basic home to a smart home with the installation of various additions.

For example, adding security can be as simple as installing a doorbell with remote access to a security camera. Solar and motion detecting security lighting can be installed manually in minutes to the exterior of your home. Lighting and temperature controls are available via voice-activated digital assistant through devices such as Google Home, Amazon Echo, or the Apple Home Pod. These upgrades are as easy as changing a light bulb and installing a new thermostat. If you care to add morphing your home into a smart home to your list of home remodeling, the possibilities are absolutely endless.

An Expert's Insight

While searching for a remedy for the older person living alone, I sought out a "smart home" expert and found Jake Wing. At 17, Wing started taking a great interest in electronics and launched it into a career as a technician. Later, Wing became a longtime associate for ADT, a home security company, at its headquarters in Pennsylvania (Wing, personal communication, May 2, 2019).

Wing currently works for America's Security in Mesa, Arizona, where he coordinates with past, present, and future homeowners to integrate smart home technology into their homes. With 27 years of experience with security and smart home devices, Wing is continually refreshing his knowledge due to the exponential growth of smart home advances.

"A smart home is a home where multiple devices interact with each other and run from a single source or platform," Wing said.

"For example, the Pulse ADT system allows you to combine home security with various other home functions such as temperature and lighting."

Wing said these devices have recently also begun to interact with Amazon's Alexa, an artificial intelligence device that doubles as search engine. Interaction between devices allows monitoring and management from inside and outside the home. All the features of such systems can be accessed via "smart phone" with an application called Alarm.com, according to Wing. He said that this is the most commonly used app for this purpose.

Wing also described a new technology called Z -Wave mesh networks in which the security and its support systems can run independently of wireless connection for encrypted, secure, and faster services.

Basically, smart homes are needed for convenience, security, and early warning systems, according to Wing. He said this is especially true for families of independent minded senior citizens living alone.

Detection systems range from smoke and heat sensors to motion and fall monitoring. Wing explained that a system of indoor and outdoor motion-sensitive, speaker cameras can send immediate notification of an abnormality. These encrypted messages are sent only to authorized family members.

For example, Wing said if a person falls alone in their home and is not conscious, a gyro- type, wearable device will activate the system without them having to press a button. An intermediary company such as ADT would be notified and can speak to the person via the wearable keypad which has two-way voice capabilities. In the case of unconsciousness, no response from the client would initiate an alert for emergency medical help and a message would also be sent to the family.

Wing also described a scenario of a burning pot on the stove initiating a similar response due to photo electric sensors which work through a combination of heat and smoke detectors.

A future of independence in your own home is a viable option, especially with the use of these products according to Wing. He said concerned families will benefit from the new technology as well by giving them peace of mind and keeping them apprised of the wellbeing of their loved ones.

Any home, regardless of its age, can wirelessly use the smart technology with simple non-invasive devices according to Wing. He said some of these devices include plug-in outlets, smart thermostats, and doorbells with cameras. Occupants can preview visitors and/or deliveries while simultaneously turning on lights or opening a garage for access. All of this can be done in the comfort of your home's preset temperature from your favorite chair.

To evaluate your home needs professionally, Wing suggested contacting a dealer such as ADT globally. Locally in Arizona, you can also contact America's Security Company. Investing in upgrading to a smart home can open many new possibilities for enjoying a lifetime in your own home.

Smart Kitchens

Kitchens are focal point of home and family activity. In technological terms, your kitchen is the central processing unit of your home. Upgrades in the kitchen can allow you to access this "CPU" from anywhere inside or outside of your home. As you age, mobility will become a factor in running your home. A smart kitchen will ease the difficulty of maintaining physical access to this area.

Your physical limitations may hinder your access to basic needs such as cooking, cleaning, and stocking your kitchen; a smart kitchen can function on its own. Even today, smart appliances limit the need for personal assistance. For example, modern refrigerators can take stock of their contents and alert you of needed supplies. From a central "Smart Hub," you can order delivery of these items to create a revolving food store. Other capabilities of smart refrigerators are temperature and humidity controls. You may choose to use your refrigerator as a centralized processing unit for your entire home as it is possible to add a family calendar, a to-do list, and access to third-party devices such as security and intercom systems among other applications.

Other smart appliances such as stoves, ovens, microwaves, and dishwashers now offer on-demand control from any room in your house. Your real life caretaker can prepare a meal and load a dishwasher for you to set to power on and off at will. Therefore, when your companion returns after their respite, the kitchen will be clean, stocked, and ready for dinner.

Smart Tidying

When tidying your home becomes difficult for you, you can now rely on technology to assist you in cleaning up. You can rely on robotic vacuums and wet mops to roam your home at your command. You may have already heard of the Bissell® Smart Clean® Robot Vacuum, the iRobot® vacuum, the Roomba® Robot Vacuum, Samsung POWERbot™, Bravva® Robot Mop, or others.

There are robotic mechanisms which exist today to provide a variety of other services. No longer must you worry about disinfecting bathrooms, window washing, cleaning cat litter, or even shoveling out gutters. Consider the ScoopFree® litter box by PetSafe, the Omega Paw Roll'N Clean cat litter box, or the Cat Genie® which allows for a clean litter box with little work from you. The Looj® 330 Gutter Cleaning Robot by iRobot tackles this dangerous job for you.

"Researchers at the Houston Technology Center created the Xenex® to address disinfection of rooms, such as a bathroom. The Xenex® is a cleaning robot which uses 'pulsed xenon UV' light to disinfect rooms. Serbot AG, of Switzerland, is one company that has developed a line of robots designed to clean the glass outer surfaces of skyscrapers. They have two models, the Gekko and the CleanAnt."

Through my research I have found there are many more

inventions to come. Living a lifetime in your own home is possible and the future holds great promise to ease your maintenance worries. These inventions will leave you ample time to relax in your personal sanctuary.

Smart Bathrooms

Bathrooms of the future will contain greatly improved technology to adjust for your needs as you age in place. Safety and comfort measures have been taken into consideration when it comes to today's smart bathrooms.

According to the online article "Preventing Senior Falls in the Bathroom" by *NewsUSA*, "More than one in three seniors over age 65 fall each year, and the National Institute on Aging (NIA) says 80 percent of these falls are in the bathroom" (2012). For this reason, safety in the bathroom will be of the highest priority to prevent hospitalization due to a fall.

With smart technology safety measures in the bathroom, you will have tackled the risk of slipping, falling, and beyond. Take for example, the Tornado Body Dryer, a gentle, safe, in-shower, full-body drying unit that is mounted inside of your shower to completely dry your body. At the same time, the Dri-Eaz Dri-Pod

Floor Dryer-F451 will dry your floor with a high pressure airflow. For a more high-tech solution, the ILIFE Floor Washing Robot will mop, scrub, and dry your bathroom floor just in time for you to step out of the shower or tub. Considering the combined one-time cost of these products, it is far cheaper than one hospital visit.

Comfort measures in designer, high-tech toilets can adjust the temperature and softness of the toilet seat to aid fragile joints. They are able to also provide self-flushing and cleaning as well as heated seats and foot rests. The Numi intelligent toilet with KOHLER Konnect® is just one of many high-tech designs in Kohler's arsenal. Smart mirrors and lighting are available to adjust for your visual requirements. From beginning to end, your bathroom experience will effortlessly ensure comfort and safety in your own home.

Smart Bedrooms

The bedroom has not been left out of the smart home revolution. You can outfit your home to be smart and fit with smart beds. According to TechCrunch, the Luna Smart Bed Cover can adapt any bed into a smart bed (Ha, 2015). Smart beds are able to increase your comfort and sleep quality.

On their own, smart bed mattress covers can adjust lights, music, and zone temperatures of bedding. Also, as a result of their fit technology, smart beds are able to function as a biometric tracker of your heart rate, respirations, and the quality and quantity of your sleep. Therefore, sleep apnea and other medical conditions experienced during sleep can be properly diagnosed. Depending on your setup with third-party appliances, smart beds can even adjust your home appliances such as lighting and coffee makers.

Biometric monitoring during sleep can be especially helpful to reduce doctor's visits and provide up-to-the-minute personal health information. The future of smart beds will also include adjustments for the incline, firmness, and temperature for maximizing sleep quality during the night. Once you're home from the hospital, or, for night to night sleep quality, these beds can significantly improve your recovery and healing. Such restorative sleep leads to a more productive day.

The Future of Health Monitoring & "Fit Homes"

It is always concerning when aging parents want to stay in their own home. Lots of anxiety and guilt on behalf of family and friends surrounds this decision. Your independence in your own home need not be dependent on these emotions. Technology has caught up with the desires of an aging population.

Multitudes of monitoring devices can ease the worries your family and friends. Products such as Mobile Help® and Bay Alarm Medical® provide medical alert services through AT&T. Great Call® is another service affiliated with Verizon mobile. These medical alert services can be joined with cellular services for mobility or to landlines. There is usually an associated monthly fee but no long-term contract.

These monitoring devices can function from a central wall button unit or a personalized watch or pendant. They provide information to the third-party service-provider which can immediately detect falls using GPS monitoring. Accurate, up-to-the-minute health monitoring is included with the watch or pendant option. Health monitoring includes measurement of sleep anomalies, weight, and vital signs such as blood pressure, heart rate, and blood oxygen concentration.

These devices represent an upgraded method to carrying a smart phone due to their constant connection with the body. Reviews of these and other devices can be found at Consumer Reports online at www.consumerreports.org/medical-alert-systems/how-to-choose-a-medical-alert-system/. Other services are expanding based on these medical alert devices.

According to an online piece by Home Health Care News, Best Buy is targeting seniors and baby boomers with new health monitoring technology.

The "retailer has joined well-known brands offering technology solutions to senior care, rolling out its Assured Living program— a sensor-based notification service utilizing a slew of devices, such as motion, bed, chair and door sensors; Wi-Fi enabled doorbell cameras; and smart locks and thermostats that can pair up with the senior resident's smart phone" (Calma, 2017).

"In Denver, the technology is used in tandem with a wellness coach sponsored by health insurance provider UnitedHealthcare to supply the resident and caregivers/family members with a personalized wellness program, coupled with health education and access to other resources, including transportation, meal preparation/delivery services and home health and rehabilitation services"(Calma, 2017).

In addition to monitoring, other healthcare resources are also available from the home. A large number of insurance companies employ teladocs and telemedicine such as American Well, Doctor on Demand, and Interactive M.D. A newer subsection of telemedicine includes specialists. Such services offer telephone or video conferencing with doctors, nurses, and specialists for on-call services and/or second opinions.

These doctors communicate in several ways. They use email, phone, text messages, and video chat. This is a win-win-win situation. It allows doctors to work remotely and more efficiently, it allows you anytime access, and it lowers the costs to insurance companies. Integrating the services of remote monitoring and remote diagnosis will ease your top concerns. This allows you freedom to focus on higher priorities such as family and friends.

The cost of these services is substantially lower than a traditional doctor's visit for the insurance company and is often more convenient for the patient who doesn't have to leave the comfort of their own home. These in-home consultations typically range from free to $50 per visit depending on your insurance coverage. More personalized 24/7/365 care may include a monthly fee. In following the earlier tenet of know thy healthcare, first investigate the services recommended by your plan and the cost for using them. You can learn more about online or telemedicine consultations at www.vsee.com/online-doctor-consultation/.

The Future of Entertainment

Entertainment in the form of books, music, video, and gaming will become a staple for your future home. These forms of entertainment will change in format and delivery. A well-designed smart home will be prepared for this. With a predetermined plan, a smart home can be wired for up-growth in the entertainment sector. Thus, the influx and outflow of information can be independently controlled. No institution could provide such personalization.

Currently, we have a surprising number of options. Unlimited digital cable, streaming, recording, ultra-high definition, and satellite services precede even more innovation. Each day companies are adding to and personalizing these options even further. Though, it still seems that the hunger for entertainment cannot be satisfied. Consumer-driven appetites will demand more realistic and interactive options.

It's difficult to predict the future of entertainment. The insights I have gathered from research have shown a trend towards integration of entertainment to involve all of the senses.

The online article "Entertainment of the future" by Focusing future stated that "Infographics, content summarized with graphical representations, keywords, and concise data, are so easy to consume." The article shows that the future will unlock the maze of entertainment access. Sight, sound, touch, taste, and possibly, smell will entice you toward the new information superhighway" (2018).

Sony has already launched a Project Morpheus VR Headset for PlayStation 4. Morpheus is set to deliver a sense of presence, making the player feel as though they've stepped inside the world of a game according to Sony's official website. The headset will bring us to alternative reality (Entertainment of the future, 2018).

Not Impossible Labs debuted Vibrotextile™ technology that translates sound onto the skin through vibration, allowing users to feel the nuances of a music-listening experience, according to the online piece "Music: Not Impossible Provides a Glimpse into the Future of Music" by CISION PR Newswire.

"The product creates an experience and opportunity for creative expression that constitutes a new art form for all," the article stated. "Music: Not Impossible is a combination of wearables, hardware, software and wireless tools. The battery-powered wireless wearables include two wristbands, two ankle bands, and a harness; each element receives complex polyphonic musical expressions across the skin. Wearers may adjust the intensity of vibrations, which are visually represented via colorful LED lights" (Music: Not Impossible Provides a Glimpse into the Future of Music, 2018).

Setting up your home of the future will involve integration of these delivery systems. I can only speculate the required features. I'm envisioning an entertainment superhighway of holograms and robotics. I can imagine the fluid process of media exchange. This enables each individual to interact with video, audio, and written material to suit their manner of learning. Specialized equipment will slowly make these changes more palatable, but the ultimate goal is freedom and independence from a one-size-fits-all entertainment.

An article by RocketSpace online predicts future changes in entertainment ranging from humanlike emotional intelligence to full sensory and social interaction (Wu, 2017). Entertainment will incorporate other needs for a great home life. Physical activity, socialization, and learning will intermingle. I'm speculating that these interactions will augment human interactions and create a new reality.

Enjoying a lifetime of entertainment in your own home seems most exciting. Our connections will flow effortlessly even as our abilities may become impaired. Social interaction and family interaction will be enhanced by media technology. Remaining relevant and knowledgeable will help us grow at any stage in life. Resources abound. The future of entertainment in our own home will outshine any institutional setting.

Innovations throughout your lifetime will continue to swell. I've come to realize that this information needs to be digested slowly and it evolves continually. While the previous chapters can be quantified more concretely, futurology is an ever-changing process. By combining social, physical, and technological upgrades, your future home will set the foundation as your place to settle in comfortably as you age.

7

PUT IT IN WRITING,

LEGAL, SAFE & SECURE

The Story of My Parents

The call was formidable, yet I know that it would be inevitable. It came from my father who said, "Your mother is in the hospital again, fourth time in the past four months. She had another seizure and I don't know what to do. We have all these new medications. I wish they could tell me something."

I live in Arizona which is 2,500 miles away from my parent's home in Rhode Island. After this phone call from my father, I could sense the panic and confusion stemming from these seemingly unending hospitalizations of my mother. She began having seizures at the beginning of the year for no apparent reason. My father was inundated with several changes in medication for her and no explanations. I knew that a trip to Rhode Island was imminent and now I needed to watch and wait for a proper time.

Ten days later he announced, "She's coming home today. She needs physical therapy. She's not steady on her feet and she's very nervous. She knows she can't remember things."

By the second week, my father told me, "The visiting nurses are coming. Will they wash the dishes and clean?"

I instructed him, "No, they will come two to three times a week for a few weeks to do physical therapy and evaluate her."

Disappointed, he responded, "We will manage."

At week three my father informed me, "I got information from the social worker at the visiting nurses' agency. She will help me. Your mother is very nervous, and she can't remember things."

A week later he told me, "We need help. The social worker didn't even call me back. I'm going to the senior center. They will help me."

My father was getting impatient for help with my mother. He was not the usual caretaker and all of these medications were confusing. She seemed like a different person because her memory was lapsing, and her balance was not improving. She was not able to perform her usual activities of daily living. At this point, the physical complications were outweighed by safety needs of 24/7 monitoring. My father was getting impatient for responses from the social worker and others who promised to help them. There was no stress relief.

After roughly one month my father called me again. Reality had begun to set in. He asked, "Who is paying for this? We need help. Anna has the boxes; the ones your mother keeps with all the papers." Anna is a very close neighbor and longtime friend of my parents who lives around the block within walking distance from my parent's house.

I kept in close contact with Anna by phone to get the details of how they were managing. It was very helpful to have a third-party providing me with a realistic viewpoint of the situation. This was partly because my parents were so stressed; they were unable to fill me in on the details. Anna was the best advocate a daughter could have ever hoped for. Even today, she gives me a minute-by-minute detailed account of how my parents are managing. I will be forever grateful for her insightful objectivity of their reality.

At the two-month mark my father called to say, "She had another seizure, so they are sending her to a neurologist. She is more confused, and they said they would need to change the medication again. I lay them out for her one dose at a time."

Every time I spoke with my father, I realized that he was being a great caretaker. But I also realized what a challenge this was for him. He had health issues of his own and the usual balance of responsibilities in his home created were becoming unbalanced. I continued to keep in contact with them often and followed up with Anna for the details.

As a nurse, I was able to talk them through changes in medication and the expectations of her treatment and recovery. My husband and I were working full-time and I felt some guilt about not making more frequent trips to Rhode Island. When my children were younger and I worked part-time, it was easier to obtain time off to travel. We made frequent phone calls to provide support and we realized that my father was managing well at this time. Again, it was a time of watching and waiting.

At the five-month mark, I received an unexpected call from Anna. Usually, I initiated the calls to Anna. She stated calmly, "Your dad's in the hospital and he will be there until Monday." It was Friday and I immediately was concerned.

"How is he doing?" I asked. "Who is taking care of my mother? Who is giving her medications?" Anna reassured me that my mother could stay with her until Monday and she would manage her medications.

In the back of my mind, I had foreseen that his health would create an emergent situation for them both, but it was a reverse adjustment for me, as their daughter, to overrule my father in any circumstance. My father had always been a strong paternal figure and was very capable. Now, reality had smacked me into action, an emergent visit was needed. I arranged for a flight to visit my parents in Rhode Island.

An Emergent Visit

Before I arrived, I was assured by Anna that my father was determined that *"Fur was going to fly."* However, I knew better. I was very aware that my parents were adults and would make their own decisions. My plan was to offer some solutions for them to get the help they needed. I did not want to become an overbearing daughter of a "sandwich generation." Respecting my parent's wishes was top priority.

When I arrived, they were very excited to see me but, as warned, my father was up for a fight. He had not stayed in the hospital but one night and, now that he was feeling better, he was back to himself. We went out to dinner to catch up and I found him warming to my suggestions. I realized that my mother had managed the structure of their retirement planning, though, at this time, she was unable to do so. Then came the dreaded "box."

Once we settled into what was before us, my father awarded me with the box of documents my mother kept in strict order. These documents included a lifetime of proof ranging from birth to marriage and beyond. I estimated it to contain more than 1,000 pages. Now I knew what I would be doing all week. After sifting through birth certificates, immunization records, marriage certificates, insurance policies, income tax forms, and a multitude of random papers, I was overwhelmed. No longer could I look at dates, clauses, exceptions, and memorandums. I divided the box into piles of essential and nonessential. I arrived at the copy store with a box and left the store with 381 collated pages to review at home.

My goal for this visit was to arrange care at home and that was accomplished. The" box" was far more daunting than any other task I encountered. Little did I know that I would become a master at legal jargon and insurance. It also turned out that my mother had an affinity for opening savings accounts wherever she could get a toaster so consolidating their accounts also complicated the hurdles I faced during this visit.

When I arrived home, the story continued and continues today. I am working to organize and streamline their retirement care plan. My visit culminated in an urgency to add this last chapter to my book.

Don't Fear "The Box"

Each generation has its way of dealing with its lifespan and our forefathers could never have predicted the future. Long gone are the days when extended families intimately knew each other's wishes and personal stories. A new generation of transient, and sometimes fractured, family life has given way to less than casual responses to emergencies. Changing demographics make it difficult to communicate on the same level of familiarity families once had.

Therefore, to ensure things go as you would like, put it in writing and keep it safe. Make it legal and secure to guarantee your wishes are granted. An organized system for stating your intentions can range from the dreaded "box" of papers to a system of notarized documents scanned into a complex computer program. Any method of organization is appropriate as long as it is accurate and legally binding.

Decisions, Decisions, Decisions

Contemplating serious decisions regarding your future requires much thought and organization. Profound reflection should precede these decisions; however, to ease your anxieties, these decisions are fluid and need not be set in stone. Circumstances change and your plans can be changed also. Factors to consider include responsibilities to family members and friends, your changing health status, and your legacy. Legacy takes into account the succession of your achievements, possessions, and bequests to others.

As you are taking time to thoughtfully reflect on your legacy, the gathering of this information will prompt you to be decisive. It is difficult to tackle this task in one round. Therefore, proceed with these activities over a period of months or whatever time is appropriate to your situation. It is like cleaning your house. The project is always there yet never feels completed. So, when preparing to enjoy a lifetime in your own home, get organized with your documents. Once all your decisions are made you should consult a lawyer or legal representative with whom you are familiar.

Steps to Success

1. Take substantial time to evaluate trusted relationships throughout your lifetime. Personally reflect on the legacy you want to leave for the future and how you want to be represented. Take some time to organize your thoughts on these matters now.

2. Discuss your expectations with your significant other and family members.

3. Write a list of your priorities and the tactics you wish to implement. Divide your wishes into categories: delegation of personal responsibilities, management of assets, and advanced directives. Use focus and creativity in an organized account of your wishes.

Gathering Information

1. **Banking and Investment Records**. Ensure you have all the information together for your loans, mortgages, and/or titles to all properties and vehicles in order.

2. **Digital Footprint**. Make a list of usernames and passwords to access computers, email, social media accounts, and other important digital assets.

3. **Legal Documents**. Gather and neatly file all insurance policies, life agreements (marriages, divorce, custody, prenuptial agreements, living trusts, etc.). Also consider putting together a power of attorney in the event that you suddenly become unable to handle your own business and decisions.

4. **Make Your Wishes Known**. Plan out your advance directives such as living wills, Do Not Resuscitate (DNR) orders, medical power of attorney, and other medical orders. Put them in writing and have them notarized or documented by an attorney.

Banking and Investment Records

Approach your banking and investments with the similar process you did for home care. Maintain a list of your accounts, their locations, and your contacts for each. Include usernames and passwords on this list.

Depending on the complexity of your accounts, consider consolidation for ease of use. For example, in my own situation my parents did not set up computerized access to their accounts. If my father wanted to know his bank balance, he drove to the bank and requested a paper copy. This complicated the process for me to pay his bills if needed. With his permission, we consolidated all accounts into one main bank, and I set up online bill pay for myself to access it in an emergency.

With the online bill pay in place, I was able to manage his bills if he were to be admitted to the hospital. He still chose not to use this service but left it available to me. This would ensure that my mother would continue safely in their home without worry of interrupted service or penalties. Whatever your financial circumstances, simplification and consolidation will make it easier to obtain help when needed.

Check with your local bank to investigate the services they provide. Automatic bill pay and online banking or online bill pay with notification can ease responsibilities in a time of crisis. I do, however, *want to warn you about giving automatic withdrawal access* to a checking or savings account. Any company which has automatic withdrawal access to your accounts can charge penalties and interest to their bills in the case of a dispute. It opens your accounts to possible inappropriate access or fraud. Small overlooked payments without notification can include magazine subscriptions, gym, club and sports memberships. Any attempt to fix these deductions will be met with great difficulty. It is much easier to reverse a faulty credit card charge. In addition, a credit card company will halt payment and help you with any disputes.

Organizing your finances, investments, and debts may seem like a monstrous task. When you start inquiring into your total assets, you will find that the process is easier when you use technology to your advantage. Most banking institutions have software applications which translate all your questions into answers. As a result, they can be integrated into pie charts and portfolios. A banking associate can assist you in devising a format that works best for you.

Keep in mind, the goal is simplicity. When your friends or family members step in to assist you, present the whole story. After all, you have worked hard towards these goals. Take credit and present an all-inclusive plan. Most of us have an idea of how our money flows. Despite the complexity of our finances, they can be made legible to others as well.

Loan Documents, Mortgages, and Deeds

Be sure to include other documents such as outstanding loan agreements and mortgage agreements in your organized file. If you have paper documents such as titles and deeds, scan them into your computer in addition to keeping the originals. This will make viewing easier and ensure they are transferable electronically.

Continue to consolidate all your records including investments. This will mean taking stock of all your assets. Include a list of all real estate, business ventures, stocks, bonds, 401Ks, and others. If such investments and money go unclaimed, after a period of time they are turned over to the state. You can find out if your state is holding money owed to you by searching online at www.usa.gov/features/free-official-sources-to-find-unclaimed-money (USAGov, 2017).

Regarding other assets, search your records for due pensions, and retirement accounts at previous employers. Other sources of income may include inheritances and cherished family heirlooms. Depending on the extent of your portfolio, combining a list of all assets may take significant time.

Consult with your financial planner about whom, when, and with what limitation you want to give access to your accounts. This is particularly important with investment accounts, IRAs, and other significant assets. I suspect that you would want your heirs to continue with the process of handling your money as you have done in the past. For this reason, consulting professionals and writing a plan is imperative.

Physical Assets

Leave no stone unturned. Your loved ones will need to be privy to every asset and source of income available to care for you. Draw in all the loose ends. Investigate past resources which may have been overlooked. These include storage facilities, bank security boxes, owed money, and profit from silent partnerships. Gather together items in your home which may have value. Books are available such as *The Life-Changing Magic Tidying Up* by Marie Kondo and *Swedish Death Cleaning* by various authors which will help you sort your belongings. Again, this is a hierarchical process to present your true legacy.

During times of crisis, your relationships will be the priority. Sharing concise knowledge with your loved ones will further build these relationships and demonstrate that you cared enough to plan ahead. Presenting your preparations in an uncomplicated format shows thoughtfulness. Your friends and family will be appreciative, especially, in a time of crisis.

Planning things in advance allows time and space for you and your loved ones to focus on more meaningful priorities. These steps will assist you in alleviating the frantic arrangements and anxieties that often accompany such trying times. Your loved ones will appreciate your intent, planning, and forethought. You can find a list of additional resources at the end of this book to further assist you.

Digital Footprint

Fortunately for me, my parents did not participate in the digital age. Usually, this is not the case. I realized this would be a problem for my own children. After years of logging on to every site and every app of interest, I lost hold of my own digital footprint. After digging through piles of scrap papers and lost notes on my smart phone, I began the process. I managed to regain many of my usernames and passwords. More work is still to be done.

Rebuilding my digital footprint became a larger task than

consolidating my assets. The reason stems from losing sight of this new phenomenon. Most websites and applications require account setups. And, it is now common knowledge that each account should have a unique and complicated password. Logging on, checking in, and posting notifications have become part of daily life.

A password manager can help you to keep all your logins and passwords safely managed in one place. There are free and paid password managers online. A few free or low-cost options include Dashlane, Sticky Password, and Password Boss.

As you trudge through gathering usernames and passwords, you will notice a pattern. At every site there is an option to reclaim your password if you have forgotten it. The option usually refers back to your original email or your phone number. Obviously, this presents an enormous problem if those have changed. As your needs in your own home increase, you may be unable to access your phone or email easily. It is imperative that at least one trusted caregiver has access to these.

A close friend of mine suffered an unexpected stroke. As I usually contacted him by phone, I was concerned with his unresponsiveness. Most strokes occur quickly and without warning. He was on vacation and slumped over during a meeting. His friends took action to get him emergency medical assistance. However, left behind were his phone and computer. Luckily, his brother was present. He collected his belongings yet was unable to access either of them, so dozens of calls went unanswered.

By the time his brother unlocked his phone and computer, his friends were in a panic. When his brother returned my call, he notified me that he was in the hospital. Fortunately, my friend recovered from his stroke and was able to return to work.

I learned from this experience. I would allow one trusted friend or relative the ability to access my digital lifelines. This would enable quick communication among friends and reduce panic among relatives. Also, any security breaches of any personal websites or applications would give notification on a phone or laptop. A stroke or illness can put your life in chaos. My friend lost control of everything. With his friends unable to contact him, he had also lost his support system and his security was in jeopardy. For some, establishing trust in others is a bold move. But consider the alternative. A hacker could eventually access your personal devices. It is better to have a trusted friend easily step in to assist you.

Your digital life expands further than you could ever imagine. You can limit access by setting up security within your accounts. Limit the flow of information to other sites and the viewing of information to other people. Unsubscribe to notifications as you become disinterested in them. Consolidate your information as much as possible. Another giant task is at hand.

I have discovered a method to tracking my usernames and passwords. Previously, I stored them on my phone. Then I realized my phone could fail, be lost, or stolen. I now store all my usernames and passwords on paper and on a thumb drive. By changing my method of tracking, I had left a copy accessible to my trusted loved ones. I have advised them of its existence. Thus, they have an automatic path to assist me.

Aging in place is an ongoing process of trust and planning. None of the activities in these chapters need to be done immediately, but in preparation to set up your future for a life in your own home, reflect upon them. Enjoying a stress-free, abundant life in your own home is possible. Keep in mind your goal of avoiding institutional life. Freedom lies in independence and independence requires organization.

Insurance Policies, Life Agreements, and More

This portion of your organization can be very complicated. *Begin by gathering all of your documents and life agreements.* As complicated as life becomes, gathering these documents may take some time. As I said earlier, this is a process. Think of it as a marathon rather than a sprint. Similar to health insurance, this will be an education and build awareness of your situation. But for now, concentrate on just gathering legal documents.

Just as I had spent a solid week sifting through legal documents from my parents, you will now have a similar project. Legal terms, riders, and clauses complicate these documents. Often there are summary pages to assist you. I would suggest making copies of the summary pages for your loved ones. Remember to include all insurance policies and life agreements such as marriage, divorce, custody, prenuptial, living trusts, and other documents. It is important to contain all your documents in one location for ease-of-use.

Many of these documents may change over time and it is important to keep up on the changes. Particularly significant are the cases of divorce and custody agreements. These agreements have a lifelong impact; thus it is crucial that your family and friends who will assist you are aware of the agreements you have in place. This way there will be no confusion in your care and continued business carried out by family members and friends. Remember, life crises lead to potentially lost independence and maintaining independence in your own home is the goal.

After you've gathered your documents, I would recommend scanning the summaries into the computer and saving them on a thumb drives or to a Google drive online that you can share with others. Personally, I save all important documents on an external hard drive which has plenty of storage. Depending on how much information is involved, check the amount of storage you will need. This will result in easy access for your family. Digital backup copies in addition to paper copies are doubly secure.

Hospitalizations often occur without warning. Case managers, nurses, and social workers will have many questions to plan your follow-up care. Organizing your documents will help. In these instances, family members can provide updated information if you are unable to do so. This is specifically important when it comes to insurance. As a case manager, I worked closely with social workers. If a patient's condition rendered them with a decreased level of consciousness or confusion, we needed to reconstruct their puzzling insurance policies. In some cases, no family members were available which made the task that much more difficult.

Thousands of patients passed through our hospital weekly. Each case came with a baffling and usually tragic story. Case managers and social workers are pressured to expeditiously find placement for patients. Thus, the more correct information provided to the hospital means more rapid results in advanced discharge. For instance, if you have a long-term care policy in place there are many benefits which will enable you to return immediately home. Long-term care policies may have been purchased much earlier in life. Perhaps their benefits had long been forgotten, but these policies can be activated at the time of discharge.

Long-term care policies can offer immediate homecare services not covered by health insurance. If your recovery care requires 24/7 assistance, such policies can be helpful. Your case manager and social worker will be assured that you will be safely discharged. Without knowledge of your insurance policies, you would likely be directed towards an institution. In summary, follow the basic rules of home care. Know thy health insurance.

Life agreements can also come into play. Concerning these documents, it is relevant to know who has the decision-making capacity for you. A social worker will be investigating your durable and medical powers of attorney. I have seen many family members appear at the bedside only to find that they do not have the authority to make decisions for my patients. The hospital requires legitimate, notarized documents to determine your plan of care. If these documents are not available, the state and local laws will prevail.

This is another reason to have your affairs in order. A skilled advocate at your bedside makes all the difference in your discharge plan. The ultimate goal is to get you home to recover in the comfort and safety of your own environment.

This chapter may seem tedious, but after discharging thousands of patients through the years, I found it compulsory to include it. It makes a difference even if you are only able to gather your information together and make easily accessible. Case managers and social workers are experienced in translating these documents quickly, therefore, they will respect your desire to return home.

Advanced Directives & Living Wills

"A living will, despite its name, isn't at all like the wills that people use to leave property at their death," according to *All Law* online. "A living will, also called a directive to physicians or advance directive, is a document that lets people state their wishes for end-of-life medical care, in case they become unable to communicate their decisions. It has no power after death" (Nolo, 2019).

"If you're helping someone with their estate planning (or doing your own), don't overlook a living will. It can give invaluable guidance to family members and healthcare professionals if a person can't express his or her wishes. Without a document expressing those wishes, family members and doctors are left to guess what a seriously ill person would prefer in terms of treatment. They may end up in painful disputes, which occasionally make it all the way to a courtroom" (Nolo, 2019).

In addition to a living will, another legal document you will want to consider is a durable power of attorney or a health care proxy. These documents legally authorize someone (an assigned agent), to decide on your behalf should you become incapacitated in some way. Such documents also allow someone to handle your business such as accessing accounts, investments, and handling your matters such as utility bills.

Your Five Wishes

Five Wishes is a simply legal advance directive document written in everyday language that everyone can understand. It acts as a living will and allows people to decide how they wish to be cared for and treated at the end of life. According to fivewishes.org, it has become the most popular living will in America with more than 30 million copies in circulation (Five Wishes, 2019). The "five wishes" include the following:

Wish 1: Person I Want to Make Care Decisions for Me When I Can't. This should be someone you trust who knows your wishes for the care you want to receive and is willing to accommodate your healthcare plans.

Wish 2: The Kind of Medical Treatment I Want or Don't Want. This should outline what kind of care you wish to have. For example, do you wish to have all medical care provided to keep you alive or do you wish to have a DNR (do not resuscitate) in place?

Wish 3: How Comfortable I Want to Be. This allows you to have pain medication to keep you comfortable even if that means that you are unconscious, or do you want to bypass medication so you are cognizant at all times?

Wish 4: How I Want People to Treat Me. This outlines how you wish to be treated by family, friends, and medical staff. If there are certain people you don't wish to see or want together in the room at the same time, for example, this is the place to outline those wishes. You can also outline that people speak directly to you when providing medical information and not just to those around you.

Wish 5: What I Want My Loved Ones to Know. This is where you can leave information for your loved ones from where to locate a safety deposit box to where you wish to leave donations after your death. You may even wish to leave personal messages in this section.

Adelaide: A Story of Unplanned Guardianship

Adelaide, at the age of 94, consistently fell in her home and landed in the hospital. She lived alone and had managed her own affairs until her last fall. Nurses noticed her repetitive statements and confusion in basic tasks. They questioned her ability to return home due to suspected dementia. Her primary team of doctors ordered a psychiatric evaluation to determine if she was able to make her own decisions.

In one fated day, Adelaide lost her power to decide her future. Adelaide was very educated and spoke with a well-developed vocabulary. She authored many financial books as her prior career was in finance. She excelled in this area and was ahead of her time. As you may have deduced, Adelaide had amassed a hefty nest egg and a structured investment plan.

Adelaide spent day after day in the hospital as we as case workers tried to find her next of kin. One sister was contacted as sole support. She was not able to care for Adelaide nor did she know Adelaide's personal intentions. She also lived 500 miles away and was seriously ill at the time. We contacted her many times to expand our search for other relatives with no avail. All avenues had been exhausted. Adelaide spent Thanksgiving and Christmas at the hospital.

As her hospital days dragged on, we became very familiar with Adelaide. She was wonderfully sweet and childlike, but she deserved to chart her own future. A public fiduciary was appointed to determine this for her. Adelaide was transferred to a locked memory unit within an assisted living facility. Her worldly possessions were dispersed accordingly among an estate sale and her current residence sold. Her smart financial planning had allowed her to pay for excellent care. Adelaide was pleasantly confused by her new home.

"The appointment of a Guardian should be considered only when all other options have been exhausted. It should never be used in a retaliatory manner or as a convenience for health-care providers, family members or others. Guardianship can be an intrusive intervention in a person's life" (Public Fiduciary, 2019).

Each state government has a similar yet distinct process for guardianship.

Adelaide's situation was not unique. This is the reason why I stress "put it in writing." A written plan creates tangible resolutions while simultaneously informing others. Furthermore, notarize and legalize your wishes. Involve your family. Notify them of your intentions and where legal documents are located. Share your lawyer's contact information including their name, address, phone number, and email address.

For some unknown psychological reason, I had no difficulty in creating these documents. The difficulty came with informing my family of their existence. Approaching subjects of imminent health decisions was especially taxing. Many times, family members want to defer these discussions to another time. These are difficult subjects, but family members must eventually and respectfully yield to your wishes.

Put it in Writing

Whether it's your first or your fifth hospitalization in a row, you will undoubtedly learn new terms. Your new vocabulary will include durable power of attorney (DPoA), medical power of attorney (MPoA), and laws of surrogate decision-making, the laws referred to in your state and local chains of guardianship. Without legal documentation of your predetermined decision maker, your future will be determined by these laws.

Forms such as durable and medical power of attorney will reinforce your wishes in writing. Written documents provide the most accurate and concrete information for legal purposes. Notarized written documents are even better. Be sure they are legible and dated. It is advisable to meet with a lawyer to ensure your forms are properly written. Legal advice will also help you decipher the specific needs in your geographic area.

After all your investigative work and efforts to get things in order, it would be wise to keep your wishes legal, safe, and secure. For simplicity's sake, I would recommend designating one or two places for all of your information. For example, one set of documents could be consolidated into paper copies and another set could be scanned onto a thumb drive or other external drive. Computerized documents are easily accessible and transferable in case of an emergency. Paper documents are also valuable in case of computer failure and/or the need for original copies. Ensure all the prerequired notarizations are in order on all of your documents so they are legal and binding.

Take the first steps to choose your favorite method of storage so your work will be secure after you have gathered all your documents. Protected information can also be stored in bank safe deposit box or at a family member's home. Sometimes it is good to store your information in different locations.

Another benefit of using different locations and different forms of storage results in an added level of protection. These methods also allow access for your family members in an emergency. Consider these actions another level of emergency preparedness. Imminent hospitalization can be as devastating as the fire, flood, or earthquake. Proper storage of your documents can make your transition home from the hospital effortless for you and your family. Remember the goal is peace of mind in enjoying a lifetime in your own home.

CONCLUSION

Through my experiences as a registered nurse, I have gained compassion for patients after seeing the devastation that hospitalization can bring. I have seen all aspects of the process. During admission, stress and uncertainty often set the stage for your course. As the bedside nurse, I witnessed patients enduring surgeries and procedures which they never expected. As surprising as the hospitalization itself, the discharge plan is also often unanticipated. Pensive conversations begin. This book contains the results of those conversations.

"I never thought I would live to this age."

"How did I get here and what do I do now?"

"I just want to go home."

Most people do just want to go home. It is our safety and our sanctuary. Familiarity of our home provides respite after the stress of a hospitalization. Home is more than a place in which we reside. It is where we run our independent, private lives. It is the culmination of our lifelong dreams and experiences.

With the advice, stories, and guidelines in this book, I hope to have enlightened you to the possibilities of enjoying a lifetime in your own home. My hope was to generate the best ideas and practices towards aging in place. Apply the information you wish and ponder the rest. Preparing for the future is a process.

"Enjoying a lifetime in your own home is possible."

BIBLIOGRAPHY

"Aging in Place: A State Survey of Livability Policies and Practices." (2011). AARP. Retrieved March 10, 2019, from https://assets.aarp.org/rgcenter/ppi/liv-com/ib190.pdf.

AARP. (2019). AARP HomeFit Guide. Retrieved March 10, 2019, from https://www.aarp.org/livable-communities/info-2014/aarp-home-fit-guide-aging-in-place.html.

Bronshtein, G., Scott, J., Shoven, J. B., & Slavov, S. N. (2018, January). The Power of Working Longer. Retrieved March 31, 2019, from https://www.nber.org/papers/w24226.

Calma, C. (2017, October 04). "Best Buy Tests Home Care Monitoring Technology." Home Healthcare News. Retrieved May 27, 2019, from https://homehealthcarenews.com/2017/10/best-buy-tests-home-care-monitoring-technology/.

Cacioppo, J. T., & Cacioppo, S. (2014). "Social Relationships and Health: The Toxic Effects of Perceived Social Isolation." Social and personality psychology compass, 8(2), 58-72.

Chen, J. (2019, March 25). "Passive Income." Investopedia. Retrieved March 31, 2019, from https://www.investopedia.com/terms/p/passiveincome.asp.

Chen, J., & Murphy, C. B. (2019, March 28). "Prospectus." Investopedia. Retrieved March 31, 2019, from https://www.investopedia.com/terms/p/prospectus.asp.

Code of Federal Regulations: ADA Standards for Accessible Design. (2010, September 15). Retrieved March 15, 2019, from https://www.ada.gov/1991standards/adastd94-archive.pdf.

"Entertainment of the future." (2018, August 06). Retrieved May 27, 2019, from http://www.focusingfuture.com/me-consumer/entertainment-of-the-future/.

Five Wishes. (2019, January 1). Retrieved June 4, 2019, from https://fivewishes.org/shop/order/product/five-wishes.

Ha, A. (2015, January 27). "Luna's Smart Mattress Cover Can

Help You Sleep Better." TechCrunch. Retrieved May 27, 2019, from https://techcrunch.com/2015/01/27/luna-smart-mattress-cover/.

Hirschberg, C., Rajko, A., Schumacher, T., & Wrulich, M. (2016, November). "The changing market for food delivery." McKinsey & Company. Retrieved May 13, 2019, from https://www.mckinsey.com/industries/high-tech/our-insights/the-changing-market-for-food-delivery.

HomeAdvisor. (1999-2019). Retrieved March 15, 2019, from https://www.homeadvisor.com/.

How do deductibles, coinsurance and copays work? (2019). Retrieved April 14, 2019, from https://www.bcbsm.com/index/health-insurance-help/faqs/topics/how-health-insurance-works/deductibles-coinsurance-copays.html.

How Much Does Assisted Living and Home Care Cost in the US? (2019). Retrieved March 31, 2019, from https://www.seniorliving.org/retirement/assisted-living-facilities/.

Kent, J. (2015, April). "ADA Requirements for Kitchen Storage."

Retrieved March 24, 2019, from
https://steppingthruaccessibility.com/ada-requirements-for-kitchen-storage/.

Khalfani-Cox, L. (2017, February 14). "Can You Afford to Age in Place?" Retrieved March 15, 2019, from
https://www.aarp.org/money/budgeting-saving/info-2017/costs-of-aging-in-place.html.

Korosec, K. (2018, July 20). "Waymo's autonomous vehicles are driving 25,000 miles every day." TechCrunch. Retrieved May 13, 2019, from https://techcrunch.com/2018/07/20/waymos-autonomous-vehicles-are-driving-25000-miles-every-day/.

Kubler-Ross, Elisabeth. (1969). On Death and Dying: What the Dying Have to Teach Doctors, Nurses, Clergy, and Their Own Families.

Lambert, F. (2017, April 06). "Hyperloop One reveals 11 potential routes for the high-speed transportation system in the US." Retrieved May 13, 2019, from
https://electrek.co/2017/04/06/hyperloop-one-us-routes/.

Lambert, F. (2018, November 28). "Tesla's fleet has accumulated over 1.2 billion miles on Autopilot and even more in 'shadow mode', report says." Retrieved May 13, 2019, from https://electrek.co/2018/07/17/tesla-autopilot-miles-shadow-mode-report/.

Mahoney, J. E., Eisner, J., Havighurst, T., Gray, S., & Palta, M. (2000). "Problems of older adults living alone after hospitalization." Journal of general internal medicine, 15(9), 611-9.

Malito, A. (2018, January 22). "Delaying retirement by up to 6 months is equivalent to saving an additional 1% over 30 years." Market Watch. Retrieved March 13, 2019, from https://www.marketwatch.com/story/you-may-want-to-work-longer-heres-why-2018-01-22.

Music: Not Impossible Provides a Glimpse Into the Future of Music. (2018, September 25). Retrieved May 27, 2019, from https://www.prnewswire.com/news-releases/music-not-impossible-provides-a-glimpse-into-the-future-of-music-300718746.html.

Nolo. (2019, January 1). "What is a Living Will?" AllLaw. Retrieved June 4, 2019, from https://www.alllaw.com/articles/wills_and_trusts/article7.asp.

Pant, P. (2019, March 12). "The 50/30/20 Rule of Thumb for Budgeting." The Balance. Retrieved March 24, 2019, from https://www.thebalance.com/the-50-30-20-rule-of-thumb-453922.

Part A & Part B sign up periods. (2019). Retrieved April 14, 2019, from https://www.medicare.gov/sign-up-change-plans/how-do-i-get-parts-a-b/part-a-part-b-sign-up-periods.

Part A costs. (2019). Retrieved April 14, 2019, from https://www.medicare.gov/your-medicare-costs/part-a-costs.

Preventing Senior Falls Starts in the Bathroom. (2012, September 19). Retrieved May 27, 2019, from http://www.newsusa.com/articles/article/preventing-senior-falls-starts-in-the-bathroom.aspx.

Prince, T. (2017, September 28). "PackExpo flaunts future of packaging, package delivery." Review Journal. Retrieved May 13, 2019, from https://www.reviewjournal.com/business/packexpo-flaunts-future-of-packaging-package-delivery/.

Public Fiduciary. (2019, January 1). Retrieved June 4, 2019, from https://webcms.pima.gov/government/public_fiduciary/.

Rossetti, R. (2006, December). The Seven Principles of Universal Design. Retrieved March 13, 2019, from http://www.unitedspinal.org/.

Smartsheet. (n.d.). Retrieved from https://www.smartsheet.com/complete-collection-monthly-budget-templates.

The Audiopedia. (2017, January 22). Retrieved May 13, 2019, from https://www.youtube.com/watch?v=HilzqsplkJ0.

The Cost of Aging in Place Remodeling. (2019, January 3). Retrieved March 31, 2019, from https://www.retirementliving.com/the-cost-of-aging-in-place-remodeling.

Thomas, M. (2011, May/June). Villages Help Older People Age in Place, Stay in Their Homes Longer- AARP Th… Retrieved March 10, 2019, from https://www.aarp.org/home-garden/livable-communities/info-04-2011/villages-real-social-network.html.

Trotter, C. (2015, October 19). 8 companies shaping the future of

delivery. Retrieved May 13, 2019, from https://www.insider-
trends.com/8-companies-shaping-the-future-of-
delivery/#ixzz5ZJfeD5Gu.

USAGov. (2017, February 22). Free, Official Sources to Find
Unclaimed Money. Retrieved June 4, 2019, from
https://www.usa.gov/features/free-official-sources-to-find-
unclaimed-money.

Village to Village Network. (2019). Retrieved March 10, 2019,
from https://www.vtvnetwork.org/content.aspx?
page_id=22&club_id=691012&module_id=238482&actr=4.

What Does a Nursing Home Cost? (2019, January 17). Retrieved
March 31, 2019, from https://www.retirementliving.com/what-
does-a-nursing-home-cost.

What Does It Cost? (2019). Retrieved March 31, 2019, from
https://www.whereyoulivematters.org/what-does-it-cost/.

What Part A Covers. (2019). Retrieved April 14, 2019, from
https://www.medicare.gov/what-medicare-covers/what-part-a-
covers.

What Part B Covers. (2019). Retrieved April 14, 2019, from https://www.medicare.gov/what-medicare-covers/what-part-b-covers.

Wingler, W. (2014, June 4). Top 5 things to consider when designing an accessible kitchen for wheelchair users. Retrieved March 24, 2019, from http://www.eastersealstech.com/2014/06/04/accessiblekitchendesign/.

Wu, C. (2017, March 29). 10 Bold Projections for The Future of Entertainment: Algorithms, Immersive experiences, Virtual assistants. Retrieved May 27, 2019, from https://www.rocketspace.com/rocketspace/future-of-entertainment-report-released.

Wurtman, J.J., Ph.D. (2017, June 19). Social Loneliness May Make the Depressed Even More SO. Retrieved March 10, 2019, from https://www.psychologytoday.com/us/blog/the-antidepressant-diet/201706/social-loneliness-may-make-the-depressed-even-more-so.

ADDITIONAL RESOURCES

5 Benefits of Living in Place

Information for retirement living

Visit www.retirementliving.com

(Go to Senior Living, Aging in Place, 5 Benefits of Aging in Place)

Aging in Place General Resources

Resources for aging in place

Visit www.aginginplace.com/

Aging in Place Technology Watch

Technological innovations for making aging in place easier

Visit www.ageinplacetech.com/

Aging with Dignity

Resources, news, and advice for aging persons

Visit www.agingwithdignity.org/

American Association of Retired Persons

Find your "Home Fit Guide"

Visit www.aarp.org/livable-communities/info-2014/using-an-OT-or-CAPS.html%20-find%20your%20%E2%80%9CHome%20Fit%20Guide%E2%80%9D/

American Disability Association

A plethora of American disability design standards and regulations

Visit www.ada.gov

Eldercare Locator

Services for older adults and their families

1-800-677-1116 (toll-free)

Visit www.eldercare.acl.gov/Public/Index.aspx

Five Wishes Documentation from Samaritan Healthcare & Hospice

Documents for outlining your five wishes

Visit www.samaritannj.org/resources/5-wishes-living-will-documents/

Five Wishes for Your Legacy from Five Wishes®

Information for defining your legacy using the Five Wishes

Visit www.fivewishes.org/

Financial Advice from an Early Retiree

Financial resources

Visit www.mrmoneymustache.com/

Financial Freedom from Financial Advisor Dave Ramsey

Financial advice

Visit www.daveramsey.com/

HealthCare.gov

Check out definitions of medical devices and which are covered
by your insurance

Visit www.healthcare.gov/glossary/durable-medical-quipment-
dme/

Legal Trusts and Wills Online Forms

Easy to use legal documents

Visit www.legalzoom.com

Low Income Home Energy Assistance Program

Find local assistance for paying for your energy bills

Visit liheapch.acf.hhs.gov/get_help.htm

Medicare & Medicaid

Resources and information for accessing Medicare and Medicaid

1-800-633-4227 (toll-free)

1-877-486-2048 (TTY/toll-free)

Visit www.medicare.gov/

The National Aging in Place Council

Resources for aging in place

Visit www.ageinplace.org

National Association of Area Agencies on Aging

1-202-872-0888

Visit www.n4a.org/

National Association of Home Builders

Find a certified aging in place specialist

Visit www.nahb.org/find/searchresults.aspx?#q=Aging%20in
%20place%20specialists&sort=relevancy

National Energy Assistance Referral (NEAR)

Help finding local Low-Income Energy Office

1-866-674-6327 (toll-free) or 1-866-367-6228 (TTY/toll-free)

Email NEAR at energyassistance@ncat.org

National Institute of Health

Advice and resources for aging in place

Aging in Place: Growing Old at Home

Visit www.nia.nih.gov/health/aging-place-growing-old-home

National Resource Center on Supportive Housing and Home Modifications

1-213-740-1364

Visit www.homemods.org

New Technologies for Aging in Place – Today's Geriatric Medicine

Article about geriatric medicine and technology for aging in place

Visit

www.todaysgeriatricmedicine.com/archive/spring08p26.shtml

Senior Living

Durable medical equipment and other products and services for seniors

Visit www.seniorliving.org

Seniors to Aging in Place Technology

Participate in online chat groups, ask questions, and get answers

Visit www.care.com/community/seniors

Smart home- Home Automation Systems, Products, Kits, Hubs & Ideas

Information about smart home automation

Visit www.smarthome.com/

Tidying/Organizing

Tips and advice for decluttering, getting organized, and tidying up

Visit konmari.com/products/the-life-changing-magic-of-tidying-up

Available at www.Amazon.com

Universal Design

Features all elements of universal design including common fixes and upgrades

Visit www.universaldesign.com

Village to Village Network

Locate village to village networks in your area

Visit www.vtvnetwork.org/

What Is a Smart Home

Information about modern smart homes

Visit www.smarthomeusa.com/smarthome/

Social Media & Networking Resources for Chapter 2

Ancestry

Similar to My Heritage, this site helps you track relatives and DNA analysis

Visit www.ancestry.com/

Classmates

Revive your high school days and reach out to classmates all in one place

Visit www.classmates.com

Facebook

A truly social network to link and search for family and friends

Visit www.facebook.com

Instagram

Primarily focused on photos to share instant memories

Visit www.instagram.com

LinkedIn

A prime business networking and business to business platform

Visit www.linkedin.com

Meetup

This site directs you to live events with groups of people who share similar interests

Visit www.meetup.com

My Heritage

Discover your family history online

Visit www.myheritage.com

Next Door

A close to home site to get acquainted with your neighbors

Visit www.nextdoor.com

Pinterest

"Pin" unlimited ideas and interests to your personal page for sharing

Visit www.pinterest.com

Skype

Communicate directly with instant messaging, voice, and/or video chat

Visit www.skype.com

Snapchat

A way to share photos and videos which disappear shortly after
viewing

Visit www.snapchat.com

Twitter

An instant communication site for a more direct approach

Visit www.twitter.com

Vero

Social media site that allows you to make posts, send photos, and
ship videos to specifically chosen recipients.

Visit www.vero.co/

CPSIA information can be obtained
at www.ICGtesting.com
Printed in the USA
FSHW010955310719
60570FS